Historic Houses of Connecticut Open to the Public

H.F. Randolph Mason

The Pequot Press, Inc., Old Chester Road, Chester, Conn. 06412

Copyright © 1963, 1966 and 1973 by

THE PEQUOT PRESS, INC.

Chester, Connecticut

Note on the Third Edition

Since the publication of the last edition, the publishers have received information and photographs on thirteen additional historic houses in Connecticut that are open to the public. These are included in this edition. The center map has been revised and the numbers of the houses have been changed to match the page numbers. Also, some necessary changes have been made in the footnote information about visiting days and hours.

FIRST EDITION	1963
Second Printing	1964
SECOND EDITION	1966
Fourth Printing	1969
THIRD EDITION	1973

ISBN 0-87106-134-1

Library of Congress Catalog Card Number 73-85464

HOUSES AND TOWNS

Locations shown on numbered map in center spread.

Putnam Cottage (Pre-1700)

A scene of considerable activity during the colonial days when Israel Knapp and others of his family played host to many a famous personage in their travels by horseback or stagecoach between New York and Boston, the once famous Knapp Tavern now stands as a more peaceful abode. The old home was built between 1692, when Timothy Knapp acquired the land, and 1729 when he deeded one half of it to his son, Israel Knapp, who then ran it as a tavern.

Though a stone ell was added about 1800, the house appears today about as it did in 1779, when General Israel Putnam was a guest, but was surprised by British General Tryon and his troops approaching along the Boston Post Road. Putnam, with a small detachment of troops offered some resistance, but was forced to flee to Ft. Stanford for reinforcements. During its early days, too, one of the first Masonic lodges in the colonies held its meetings here.

Col. Herschel Adams purchased the house in 1901, and with several fellow townsmen, organized the Israel Putnam House Association and later it was turned over to the Putnam Hill Chapter DAR who have continued to maintain and restore it. Included among many antique furnishings are memorabilia from General Putnam and his family.

Extensive restoration has uncovered two rare fieldstone fireplaces and the rooms are being restored back to their original appearance. Restoration will continue.

Israel Putnam House Ass'n.   Open: Mon., Thurs., Fri., Sat. 10-5;
243 East Putnam Avenue   telephone for appointment.
Greenwich—Phone 869-8034   50¢, children under 12 free.

Bush-Holley House

Tradition has it that the Bush-Holley House was built either by a Dutch trader before 1685, or by the Town's first parson, Eliphalet Jones. Justus Bush acquired it in 1738, then his son David in 1760, who left it to his sons, Justus Luke and Dr. Ralph Isaacs Bush.

Justus Bush installed beautiful panelling c. 1740 and about 1780, David added a kitchen wing. During the Revolution Mrs. David Bush sponsored Church of England services in her home. Her portrait, painted in 1817 by William Dunlap, hangs in the parlor.

Much of architectural interest was discovered during restoration, including wallpaper bearing the tax stamp of George II, a hidden stone stairway, bake ovens and beautiful Jacobean fireplaces. The ancient barn provides an Auditorium, Art Gallery and an Exhibition Hall displaying early tools.

The property was purchased in 1882 by Edward P. Holley, who, with his wife, operated it as Holley Inn. Soon it became the center for young artists and writers, including John H. and Alden Twachtman, Lincoln Steffens, Ernest Thompson Seton, Willa Cather, Childe Hassam, Walt Kuhn, Elmer Livingston MacRae, Robert Frost, Rose O'Neil (Kewpi), Jerome Myers, Bert Liston Taylor, Louis Comfort Tiffany, Arthur B. Davies and others. Here the Association of American Painters and Sculptors was formed, sponsors of the 1913 "Armory Show."

The house is furnished with fine early American pieces and accessories, genealogical records, papers and material on modern American art.

Historical Society of the Town of
   Greenwich
39 Strickland Rd. (1 block S. of
   Boston Post Rd.)
Cos Cob—Phone 869-9849

Open: daily except Monday, 2-4
50¢, children free

Hoyt-Barnum Farmhouse (c. 1690)

Isaac Hoyt, descendant of Simon, one of the first settlers, was an early owner of the oldest structure in downtown Stamford. Its construction suggests a 1690 date. Restoration in 1962-63 has revealed the hewed posts, mortised and pegged, and wide vertical planking, chinked with clay and covered with a thick coat of oyster whitewash. Three fireplaces are also chinked with clay. Old clapboard is seen on the porch, enclosed about 1860, and elsewhere. Planking and floors are hand sawed and the handsome doors appear to be original. The dormer was added about 1930.

A single home, occupied by generations of simple, hard-working folk, it was long known as the "Widow Barnum House," "Betsy Barnum House," and "Grandma Barnum Homestead." From 1822-26 it was held by Ezra St. John or his widow, Ruhanna. It became associated with the Hoyt family again on the purchase by David Barnum. As wife and widow, Betsy Barnum Hoyt lived here for 46 years before deeding the house with 10 acres of land to Charlotte Elizabeth Ferris for the nominal sum of $100. A bequest by Mrs. Lillie Thompson Mather enabled the Stamford Historical Society to acquire the house in 1942.

Important collections include 19th century dolls, period costumes and accessories, Revolutionary and Civil War documents, 18th century household implements, 18th and 19th century carpentry and farm tools, prints, and a library of Stamford history and genealogy. There are many other exhibits of general interest. The Hoyt-Barnum Farmhouse is now on the National Trust Register of Historic Places.

Stamford Historical Society   Open: by appointment
713 Bedford Street
Stamford—Phone 323-1975

Bates-Scofield Homestead (c. 1736)

The Bates-Scofield Homestead was built about 1736 by John Bates, Jr. The business meetings of the new Middlesex Parish (now Darien) were held in this house before the new meeting house was built in 1740. The Homestead was bought by Ezra Scofield in 1825 and it was owned by Scofield descendants until 1924. In 1963 it was acquired by the Darien Historical Society and moved in 1964 to its present location.

Several wings and a front porch, all of which had been added during the 19th and 20th centuries, were discarded and the task of restoration to the mid-18th century appearance of the house was undertaken. Following extensive research by several noted architects, it was determined that the original shape had been that of a saltbox, and the roof line was restored accordingly. The interior floor plans had been changed very little and are typical of innumerable houses which were built in Connecticut in the same period. The furnishings are typical of the period from 1736 until 1825, the years of occupancy by the Bates family.

The landscaping of the grounds has been done with great care to conform to the simple manner in which planting was done in Colonial times, using only trees and shrubs popular in those days. To the rear of the wing is an herb garden which was a gift of the Garden Club of Darien and is maintained by its members.

A new wing at the rear of the Homestead houses a library with a collection of books, maps and manuscripts relating to local and state history and genealogy. It also contains a gallery where lectures and exhibits are held frequently.

Darien Historical Society
45 Old Kings Highway North
Darien—Phone 655-9233

Open: Wed. & Thurs. 2-4,
Sun. 2:30-4:30 and by
appointment.

New Canaan Historical Society House (c. 1764)

This house built about 1764 by Stephen Hanford, soldier in the French and Indian and Revolutionary Wars, stands on land granted to his great-grandfather, William Haynes, by the proprietors of Norwalk. In the early 1770's it was the principal tavern in Canaan Parish. After the death of Stephen Hanford, it became the homestead of Joseph Silliman and remained in the Silliman family until 1925. The Historical Society purchased it in 1958.

With the exception of the wing at the back, added by the Sillimans and a few minor alterations, the house retains its original appearance. Its location near the early churches in the Historic District, gives it added traditional value.

Every article in the house bears witness to the attention paid to the furnishing of a house in the colonial and post-colonial periods. The many gifts include fine, authentic furniture, rugs and a magnificent collection of pewter.

In 1960 the Society acquired the studio of John Rogers, sculptor. It now stands near the mansion and contains a representative collection of Rogers Groups. Adjoining the House and Studio is the Society Library, 13 Oenoke Ridge, which houses the extensive collection of books, periodicals, maps and pictures on local history and genealogy. Also on the property is the Society's Antique Tool Museum and an Old Printing Shop.

Historical Society House
   & Rogers Studio
33 Oenoke Ridge—Phone 966-5598
Society Library
13 Oenoke Ridge—Phone 966-9454
New Canaan

Open: Sun., Tues., Thurs.
except holidays, 2-4:30

Open: Tues.-Sat. 9:30-12:30.
Exhibits Tues.-Sat. 2-4.

Sloan-Raymond-Fitch House (c. 1757)

On land purchased from David Lambert in 1731, Alexander Sloan built the first recorded structure. He lost the property in 1734, at which time the sheriff sold it to Eliakim Elmer, blacksmith. In 1757, Clapp Raymond, captain of the militia, built the big house which today holds portraits, furnishings and ceramics of local families of the 18th and 19th centuries. The Fitch family enjoyed the house from 1846 to 1933, and the Van Wycks restored it to its Revolutionary period during their tenure until 1968.

The Wilton Historical Society received the house as a gift from Ralph Piersall of Wilton. The Sloan-Raymond-Fitch House now is the museum for its collections of antique furniture, clothing and objects of daily use in Wilton and nearby areas. It is here that the Society conducts its educational program with local schools, as well as other cultural programs and exhibits. A rear ell, famous as a Tea Room from 1938-1941, is used as a gallery for changing exhibits. The Lambert House now contains the Society's business office and historical library with extensive genealogical material on Wilton families and a fine collection of books on Connecticut and local history.

Wilton Heritage Museum   Open: Sat. and Sun. 2-5
249 Danbury Road $1.00, members free.
Lambert House   Open: Tues.-Fri. 10-5
150 Danbury Road
Wilton—Phone 762-7257

Keeler Tavern

The principal building of historic interest in Ridgefield today is the Keeler
Tavern. Originally built as a private home, it was purchased by Timothy Keeler
from David Hoyt in 1769, who turned it into a tavern in 1772. Gradually the
Tavern became the Community Center where entertainment, parties and balls
were held. Mr. Keeler, or Squire Keeler as he was known, was the first
postmaster and had his post office in the Tavern. He was also a representative
in the State Legislature for several terms. Timothy Keeler died in 1815, and
his son William succeeded him as proprietor. Other members of the family
through the generations kept the Tavern open until 1907 when it was sold
to Cass Gilbert, an architect who bought it for his home. At this time a long
wing was added to the rear of the building. The property again changed hands
in 1955, and finally was sold to the Keeler Preservation Society on July 4, 1966.

During the Battle of Ridgefield in 1777, the Tavern served as headquarters
for the Patriots and was hit by British fire. A cannonball which lodged in one
of the beams is still visible today. Because of this, the Tavern was known for
many years as the Cannonball House.

The Tavern is in fine condition, having been restored by the Society. All of
the panelling, hardware and flooring is original. Most interesting is a panelled
wall which also served as a divider, converting a bedroom (complete with
folding bed for easy storing) into a ballroom, simply by unhooking the wall
between the bedroom and hallway.

Keeler Tavern Preservation   Open: Wed., Sat., & Sun., 2-5.
  Society, Inc.   Groups by app't.
132 Main Street $1, children 25¢
Ridgefield—Phone 438-5485

Lockwood-Mathews Mansion (1868)

A splendid example of what can be accomplished by a group of determined citizens to prevent the demolition of an outstanding structure is illustrated by the work done by the Common Interest Group of Norwalk in saving the fabulous Lockwood-Mathews Mansion. Through the efforts of this organization, a city-wide referendum resulted in a decisive vote in favor of its preservation.

LeGrand Lockwood, a native of Norwalk, a builder of railroads, an executive of shipping companies, and president of the New York Stock Exchange, commissioned the architect, Detlef Lienau, to erect for him this great house in 1863; in design a combination of French chateau and Scottish manor. Sending to Europe for artists, artisans and materials, there were assembled hand cut granite blocks for the exterior, and for the interior, hand carved woodwork, inlaid marquetry, sculptured plaster ceilings, frescoed walls and ceilings, carved marble mantels with mosaic inlay, and a great many other elegant and interesting details.

The mansion was completed in 1868, but three years later, Lockwood lost his fortune and in 1876, Charles D. Mathews, New York importer, purchased the estate. His family resided here until 1938, when it was leased and later purchased by the city. Its furnishings were sold and the structure finally became a storehouse for surplus material. In 1959 plans were made for its destruction.

Privately run by The Lockwood-   Open: Sundays 1-4.
   Mathews Mansion Museum, Inc.   Special tours by request.
295 West Avenue
Norwalk—Phone 838-1434

The Captain David Judson House (1723)

On at least part of the foundation of a stone house built in 1639 by William Judson, one of Stratford's first settlers, Captain David Judson, his great-grandson, erected this substantial house in 1723. Early Judson property inventories indicate that the cellar was used as a slave quarters. It includes a large "lower kitchen" fireplace with two brick ovens, a "milk room," and now houses an extensive tool display.

The front doorway is entirely original, including the latch, typically Connecticut. The bullseye glasses in the door, which is further ornamented by a curved pediment and pilasters, are architectural features which may have been designed by the architect Thomas Salmon and inspired this type of doorway throughout the Connecticut Valley. J. Frederick Kelly's drawing of the doorway appears on the cover of the Dover edition of his book, "The Early Domestic Architecture of Connecticut."

Like many of the old houses, this one was "modernized" in the 1800's, but under expert supervision, careful restoration has been accomplished, the removal of lath and plaster revealing the fine period panelling and early fireplaces. The house is now furnished as an 18th century dwelling with original Stratford furniture and artifacts to interpret the life of the period. The upper kitchen, the borning room, the parlor and the parlor chamber have been restored to their original appearance.

At the rear of Judson House is the Catherine T. Mitchell Museum, built in 1958 and renovated in 1971-72. It houses the library, workroom, display cabinets, and storage areas arranged for the study of many collections.

Stratford Historical Society   Open: Wed., Sat., Sun.
Academy Hill btw. Main & Elm Sts.   11-5, April 1-Nov. 1 and
Stratford—Phone 378-0630   by appt. $1.00, chil. 50¢
Mailing address: P.O. Box 382

Eells-Stow House (c. 1685)

On the homelot granted him by the town, Samuel Eells built a simple dwelling about 1685. Three additions were made at different times in the 18th century, giving the house its present shape. Notable is the wide second story overhang over a coved cornice—a unique departure from the prevailing first story overhang. Also notable is the doglegged staircase in the central hall. This dogleg is repeated in the stairs from the second story to the attic.

Where once hung a rare 17th century portrait of Samuel Eells, now hangs a fine copy. "At ye Towne order," Samuel Eells transcribed the first records of 1639. Photostats of these display his handwriting. Also on view is the Nicholas Camp great chair (c. 1660), an outstanding and early example of a turned armchair in the New Haven Colony style. Nicholas Camp was one of the 44 First Planters of Milford of 1639.

Captain Stephen Stow, the 18th century owner of the house, volunteered to nurse smallpox-ridden American soldiers discharged from a British prison ship. He succumbed to the disease with forty of his charges. A state-sponsored monument to their memory is located in the Milford Cemetery.

On permanent display is the Claude C. Coffin Indian Collection. This collection of artifacts, relics and bones is considered to be the outstanding one of its kind for the Indians of south central Connecticut.

Milford Historical Society, Inc.,
  sponsor
34 High Street
Milford—Phone 874-2664

Open: Memorial Day to
mid Oct., Sun. 2-5,
holidays 10-5. Other
times by appointment.

The Colonel Stephen Ford House

Few houses are more closely associated with the founding of Milford than that of Colonel Stephen Ford, whose ancestors settled in Milford in 1646, and whose descendants lived here until recently.

It was a licensed tavern in 1710, situated on the original Post Road from Boston to New York. The house is now accredited in the Library of Congress as one of the early houses possessing exceptional historic and architectural interest. Especially noteworthy in construction, one will observe the unusual overhang of the roof on four sides, and some of the largest summer beams recorded in Connecticut.

Of outstanding interest is the original 18th century taproom, or tavern room, with its huge early fireplace, whitewashed walls and its furnishings of the period. The built-in bar, with its portcullis grate for closing at curfew time, today displays some of the finest examples of early drinking glasses, bottles, pottery, and other equipment the barkeeper used.

The atmosphere created by the early cooking utensils around the fireplace, the sausage-turned high stretcher tavern table set with pewter and wooden ware, and some of the finest in early lighting now to be seen in the house, would add greatly to the comfort and enjoyment of the fastidious traveler.

The house is of extraordinary interest in that it retains the authentic colonial heritage while being lived in today.

Mr. and Mrs. John Burk
142 West Main Street
Milford—Phone 878-6669

Open: Monday
through Saturday, 10-5

Brownson House (c. 1801)

Thanks to great local support and a firm belief in historic preservation, the Huntington Historical Society managed to save the Brownson House and move it to its present site, where it is now being readied for use by the community. The house is a simple, two-story Federal with a central chimney, five fireplaces, a handsome fan light over the front door and dentil work under the eaves. A new roof has been added, and the Society plans to have one of the rooms authentically stencilled. The small ell attached to the house had been greatly changed about 100 years ago, but now has been remodeled.

Born in 1740, Mordecai Marks was from the Jewish Colony which had come from New Amsterdam to Stratford. He eventually moved to Derby where he and Squire Elisha Mills ran a noted trading store for many years. Mordecai died in 1797 and his son, Hezekiah, inherited the property. When his father's will was proved in 1801, Hezekiah began to build the main house which took nearly four years to complete.

The family lived in the house until Silas, Hezekiah Marks' son, moved to Lockport, New York in the 1840's with a number of local families. The house was then sold by Silas to Isaac Bennett, who in turn sold it to Sheldon M. Brownson. Mr. Brownson had come to Huntington in 1852 from Kent. Mrs. Harry Buckingham Brownson was the last resident of the house, and had sold the land for a shopping center some sixteen years ago.

Huntington Historical Society   The house will be open to the
70 Ripton Road   public in the near future.
Shelton—Phone 929-5226

The Rev. Richard Mansfield House (Pre-1690)
located at 35 Jewett Street

Rector of St. James' Church for a total of seventy-two years, from 1748 to 1820, the Rev. Richard Mansfield resided in the dwelling that is now the property of the Derby Historical Society. When the house was built and by whom is not known, but it was located in what was then a thriving shipping community, and today it is one of the few old residences remaining in the lower Naugatuck Valley, and is on The National Register of Historic Places.

In 1926 it was moved across the street from its original site, but in other respects the visitors today will find it much as it appeared in the days when the venerable clergyman presided over a territory which now includes ten separate towns. It still has its saltbox form, deep brown clapboards, and massive center chimney of stone. Its double entrance door had to be replaced, but is a duplicate of the original.

Within the house are the early fireplaces, with a huge one in the kitchen, as well as the interesting woodwork and other appointments of the period. Dr. Mansfield's study contains his old desk and Bible, while other furniture of distinction is on display.

Mansfield was ordained by the Archbishop of Canterbury in England. His loyalty to that country caused him difficulties during the Revolutionary War, but following the war he was soon returned to a place of high esteem among all the residents of the area.

Derby Historical Society
P.O. Box 331
Derby

Open: by appt., call
Peter Ely 888-2628;
Mrs. James Fitzgerald
734-2300; or Raymond
Therrien 888-6610.

General David Humphreys House (1695)
located at 37 Elm Street

Built in 1695 as the parsonage of the First Congregational Church of Derby, this house was the birthplace of General David Humphreys, soldier, statesman, poet and manufacturer.

General Humphreys, a patriot who devoted his life to the service of his country, not only took part in both the Revolutionary War and the War of 1812, but also was one of the first official United States representatives to a European country, appointed by President Washington as Minister to Portugal and later, Spain. He was aide-de-camp to General Washington during the Revolutionary War.

When he returned to his native land from Spain, and retired to private life in Old Derby, Humphreys set about to preserving his birthplace. This two and one-half story, central chimney colonial house was acquired by the Derby Historical Society in 1962. The structure is in the process of restoration by the Society. An upstairs room is sheathed in feather-edge typical of the early 18th century, with a fine wide bolection molding around the fireplace. The most startling discovery was a late 17th century, almost square fireplace on the first floor, which was surrounded on two walls with floor to ceiling, double beaded, feather-edge sheathing. It has been said by several Colonial experts that when this room is restored, it will constitute a priceless, unique example of late 17th century New Haven Colony architecture. This house is listed on the National Register of Historic Places.

Although this house is still in the process of restoration, interested persons may visit the place by contacting Peter Ely, P.O. Box 331, Derby, Conn. 06418, or call 888-2628.

David Taylor House (c. 1750)

Located in downtown Danbury, the David Taylor and Dodd Houses display the collections of the Danbury Scott-Fanton Museum and Historical Society. As a part of its contribution to the Revolutionary Bicentennial Program, the Museum has recently restored the exterior of the David Taylor House, circa 1750, to its late 18th century appearance.

The interior consists of period rooms from 18th century to Victorian, and display areas of toys, costumes, Indian artifacts and military memorabilia. In 1777, when Danbury was burned by the British, the house was occupied by a Tory, and so was spared from the looting and burning. It was opened as a Museum in 1941.

Adjoining is the 1770 Dodd House which was the first hat shop in Danbury, known for many years as "The Hat City." The shop contains exhibits of early hatting methods, and displays related to the industry in its heyday.

Also on the same site is Huntington Hall, a modern exhibition building where special exhibits, varied from time to time, of New England and local history, old and new arts and crafts, and community projects may be seen.

The Ives homestead, 1780, birthplace of Charles Ives, Danbury's Pulitzer prize-winning composer and America's foremost musical pioneer, is located in nearby Rogers Park as is also the King Street one-room school house. Both are under restoration by the Museum and will be opened to the public at some future date.

Danbury Scott-Fanton Museum   Open: Wed.-Sun. 2-5,
43 Main Street   except holidays. Groups by
Danbury—Phone 743-5200   appointment. Adm. free.

"The Captain's House"

Although it had been unused for many years and had fallen almost to ruin, this plain little frame building has been restored to use as a museum by the Bridgewater Historical Society.

In 1973 it became an old fashioned country store and post office museum. Part of the original screenline from the post office in the old Center Store (now gone) was built into one corner. In another corner is a large pot-bellied stove that once heated the old Center School, with nail kegs for cracker barrel philosophers. The exhibit shelves contain goods that could be found in the country stores of long ago.

The Captain's House is well over 100 years old. Its chief distinction rests on the fact that for a short period, around 1850, this was the home of William Dickson Burnham. The story of his life reads like a tale by Horatio Alger. At 14 he was a "runaway" to sea, shipping first as a cabin boy on a clipper ship; then, at 37 he had risen to Master Mariner, holding license for command of steam or sailing ships on all seas.

Later, this "dynamic character" promoted and managed the American Hawaiian Steamship Company. His residual estate was bequeathed to this town of his boyhood, for which he had a deep affection.

The relocation and restoration of the building was a project in which the entire community took a warm and generous interest. The society was well favored by the town in having permission to locate this well furnished museum on town property, adjoining the Burnham Library and the Elijah Peck House.

Bridgewater Historical Society
Main Street
Bridgewater—Phone 354-7454

Open: Sat. afternoons
May-Sept., or by
appointment.

Elijah Peck House (c. 1820)

Once known as the "House of Brides" because so many young couples started housekeeping here over the years, the Elijah Peck House, built about 1820, is now owned by the Town of Bridgewater. It once stood on the corner of the Village Green, but was moved in 1910 a few hundred feet south to its present site, now between the Town Hall and the Burnham Library.

In 1970, the Historical Society leased the first floor for museum purposes. Volunteer help made possible a thorough refurbishing, inside and out, to make this an attractive and interesting museum. The parlor, living room, children's room, kitchen, pantry, sink room and exhibit room contain furnishings of all periods, nearly all from early Bridgewater families and their descendants.

From the living room with a spinning wheel made by the famous John Sturdevant of Bridgewater, to the children's room with a "premium doll" of Charles B. Thompson, manufacturer and mail order pioneer from Bridgewater, to the sink room with its butter making corner, the Elijah Peck House is a fascinating museum to visit. Special exhibits are shown throughout the summer.

Bridgewater Historical Society
Main Street
Bridgewater—Phone 354-7454

Open: Saturday afternoons
May through September,
or by appointment.

Home of the New Milford Historical Society

The New Milford Historical Society opened its new home to the public on July 22, 1964. The new fireproof brick building stands at the head of the Village Green on the Knapp property, joining the Knapp House. This building replaces the Boardman House on Main Street, given by the Misses Helen and Kate Boardman with an endowment to start an Historical Society.

The gallery has a group of exceptional early portraits and miniatures; other paintings acquired by the Society are outstanding among the items on display. Pottery which was once made in New Milford, furniture, glass, china, books, many beautiful costumes and numerous pieces of local historical interest are also exhibited.

The new building is joined to the Knapp House, which dates from 1815 and was owned by the Knapp family from 1838 until 1956, when it was given to the Society by Miss Mary Clissold Knapp. It consists of a Victorian living room, dining room and family room furnished with Knapp furniture and possessions. There is also a display of fine china and lusterware.

Moved from its Main Street site and adjoining the property is a brick structure erected about 1820 and purchased by the Society in 1939. This was the first bank of New Milford and Litchfield County, called the Litchfield County Bank. Here is displayed a large collection of Indian relics, including over 4,000 arrowheads found in the surrounding area.

New Milford Historical Society   Open: Wednesday and
6 Aspetuck Avenue   Saturday afternoons,
New Milford—Phone 354-3069   2-5

The Glebe House (c. 1750)

The characteristic lines and massive central chimney of the Glebe House proclaim a date of about 1750, when the small, original portion, possibly built about 1690, was enlarged. In 1771 it became the residence of John Rutgers Marshall, a priest of the Church of England, sent by the Society for the Propagation of the Gospel to be rector of St. Paul's Parish.

A "glebe" is the farm land enjoyed by a parish priest as part of his benefice. His dwelling, if in town, is a rectory. The great day in the history of this house, March 25, 1783, took place when ten priests of the Church of England met and elected Samuel Seabury to be Bishop of Connecticut. Seabury went to England where the Archbishop of Canterbury would have consecrated him, but could not because of his taking an oath of allegiance to the Crown. At Aberdeen, November 14, 1784, he was consecrated by three bishops of the Scottish Episcopal Church, thus becoming the first bishop (of any church) with a See in the United States.

This "Bestowal of the American Episcopate" was a turning point in the emergence of the Episcopal Church as an autonomous province in the Anglican Communion and is annually observed with thanksgiving.

The Glebe House has been restored and is furnished appropriately to the period, 1771-1786.

Seabury Society for the Preservation
  of the Glebe House
Hollow Road
Woodbury—Phone 263-3681

Open: Sun. & Tues. 1-5,
Wed.-Sat. 11-5; winter
4 p.m. Closed Mondays.
Donations.

The Hurd House

   The Hurd House, which is now in process of restoration by the Old Woodbury Historical Society, is located in "The Hollow" below and west of the Masonic Temple in Woodbury.
   Research indicates that this house was the home of John Hurd who became the town miller by an agreement of August 28, 1681. He died before 1690, for in that year he left the house and half of his barn to his wife Anna.
   The Hurd House in its present form consists of two half houses, combined to form a single house of two rooms on the first floor, and two rooms on the second. Early in this century, the Hurd House was a typical house with a lean-to, now commonly known as a saltbox house. The house was then modernized by the removal of the lean-to and the central chimney. However, the pitch of the roof and the size of the window openings indicated its early origin.
   The north rooms of the house originally constituted a two story house, built entirely of wood. Both the first and second floor rooms in this house still have the original horizontal pine random width sidings. There is evidence that each room had one casement window. The south half of the house was originally located near the mill site, and was moved to and joined with the earlier house about 1718. On each floor there was one room, each plastered with exposed wooden rafters. With its plastered walls and greater height, it is obviously later in date than the original house, but certainly was built before 1718.
   Restoration is progressing and the Society eventually plans to have the Hurd House as its headquarters.

Old Woodbury Historical Society   The house will be open in the
Hollow Road   near future to the public.-
Woodbury

Tapping Reeve House (1773-4)

Probably no other buildings are more closely associated with the early history of the legal profession than the Tapping Reeve House and the first law school in the country. Situated in one of New England's most beautiful towns, Judge Reeve's house was built for him in 1773-4 by Moses Seymour, about the time he established the school.

Classes were conducted under Reeve's direction until 1820, when they were turned over to Judge James Gould, who carried on until 1833. Gould entered the school as a student in 1795 and lectured there from 1798 until 1820. During those years probably more than a thousand were in attendance. Among the students were Vice Presidents Calhoun and Burr, three who served on the United States Supreme Court, six cabinet members, two United States ministers to foreign countries, 101 members of Congress, 28 Senators and 14 Governors.

The furniture includes a fine sideboard made for Judge Reeve by Silas Cheney, local cabinetmaker. The room occupied by Mrs. Reeve's brother, Aaron Burr, when a law student and another once used by the Marquis de Lafayette, are among those shown. Manuscript notebooks of law lectures, memorabilia, records of Tapping Reeve, and photographs of graduates of the school have been collected, and are exhibited in Reeve's law office, south of his house, which he built in 1784 and in which he continued to lecture to his students.

Litchfield Historical Society,   Open: May 15-Oct. 15,
   on the Green   daily 11-12, 2-5. Closed
West side of South Street   Wednesdays.
Litchfield   50¢, children 25¢

The Deacon Peter Buell House (c. 1734)

This early 18th century central chimney lean-to dwelling was the home of Deacon Peter Buell, son of Capt. John Buell, an original proprietor of Litchfield who settled there in 1721. It was raised "on a place commonly called the third Chestnut Hill" on Capt. Buell's 1724 acquisition of land. In 1734 Peter married Avis Collins, sister of the first minister and great granddaughter of the Honorable William Leete, 17th century governor of the New Haven Colony and Lt. Governor of the Connecticut Colony.

As well as becoming deacon of the first church in Litchfield, Peter served the township in many capacities and was a member of the colonial legislature. Two of his grandsons who were born in the house became noted physicians, one of whom was Dr. William Buell, president of The Connecticut Medical Society 1819-1826.

The Homestead remained in the Buell family until 1862. In 1923 ownership was regained by a direct descendant. In 1961 the house was slated for demolition, but was rescued and moved to Milton Society where it was faithfully restored. The entire house is furnished in period and lived in according to its early function. It now stands surrounded by a carefully recreated 18th century country environment.

A visit is an experience in time made possible through a unique private historical educational project called "Heritance House," Inc., the purpose of which is to present authenticated information and practical knowledge of rural family life in early New England in a totally 18th century atmosphere.

Write to: Open: by appointment only;
Mr. and Mrs. Blaine A. Cota, Jr.   brochure upon request.
Sawmill Road
Litchfield, Conn. 06759

Hotchkiss-Fyler House (1900)

In marked contrast to the simple, often rigorous life of the colonial and early Federal days, the gracious, comfortable living of a wealthy family at the beginning of the twentieth century is well reflected in the Hotchkiss-Fyler House, now the home of the Torrington Historical Society. While it may not have the appeal and evoke the same nostalgic feeling of a two or three hundred year old dwelling, it does represent an important phase in history, and recalls an era that will never be duplicated.

The house was designed by William Allen, a New Haven architect, and was constructed in 1900 for Orsamus R. Fyler, whose ancestors were among the early settlers of Connecticut. Mr. Fyler was a prominent Torrington industrialist, at one time State Insurance Commissioner, and as a dominant political figure, was chairman of the Republican State Central Committee.

Today the house remains furnished as it was when occupied by its last resident, Mrs. Edward Hotchkiss, daughter of Mr. Fyler. The richly upholstered furniture, the photographs and paintings, the lovely china and silver, the well stocked library, and all of the appointments displaying splendid taste, wealth and refinement are to be found here.

In an older house next door, the historical society has many interesting exhibits of earlier Torrington days, reminiscent of home life, as well as civic and industrial activities throughout the community.

Torrington Historical Society   Open: both houses only
192 Main Street   by appointment.
Torrington—Phone 482-8260

Gay-Hoyt House (1775)

Brick was not commonly used in the construction of early Connecticut houses, so the Gay-Hoyt House, facing Sharon's pleasant Green, is almost a rarity. Built in 1775 by Ebenezer Gay, it retains original details.

Gay was an important person in early Sharon, a mining, manufacturing and agricultural center. Tax collector, five times representative to the General Assembly and an officer in the Trainband, Gay was also a merchant and served in the Revolutionary War.

He lost his home through financial reverses and in 1793 it became the property of Isaac Hunt. Miss Anne Sherman Hoyt acquired it in 1936; she bequeathed it to the Sharon Historical Society in 1951.

The house has a center hall with end chimneys, a small elegant front porch, and fireplaces set at an angle in each room. On the first floor two rooms, named after early families Gay and Smith, contain portraits and furniture. A third room commemorates Frank Spencer, a benefactor of the society and indefatigable historian of early Sharon. This room is also the document room, where many town records are kept, the more valuable being under glass. Another room contains an unusually fine display of guns and other weapons. A room on this floor exhibits articles made in Sharon and household items. An old shed attached to the main building was recently renovated and has become the "Tool Shed" housing an outstanding tool collection of Tree Ware articles and items of the small industries of early days.

The upper floor has two rooms. One is a complete bedroom; the other shows costumes, textiles and cases of small articles. A room in the third floor attic exhibits a large loom in working condition.

Sharon Historical Society   Open: Tues. and Sat.
Main Street   2-5 from May to
Sharon   November.

Solomon Rockwell House (1813)

Solomon Rockwell, member of a prosperous iron manufacturing family, in 1813 engaged Captain William Swift of Colebrook, to construct an unusually fine mansion, sometimes called "Solomon's Temple," standing on a hillside overlooking the town. The house is distinctly Federal, with four great, carved pillars supporting the roof over the front porch, and smaller ones at the porch at the left wing. The interior contains a great deal of beautifully carved woodwork, said to have been fashioned with a jackknife, and the lovely mantels are equally attractive.

John Boyd, second owner and son-in-law of Solomon, was Secretary of State of Connecticut, town clerk of Winchester, and author of the "Annals of Winchester," one of the finest of the state's town histories. His step-daughter, Mary Pitkin Hinsdale, last member of the family to own the house, maintained here a small free library, and in her memory a local school is named.

Among the outstanding items on display at the house are a number of splendid 19th century portraits, eight of them by Erastus Salisbury Field; five are of the family of Riley Whiting, early clockmaker, and two are of the Rev. Frederick Marsh and his wife, Parnal Merrill. In addition to its attractive furnishings, many outstanding items of local interest are to be seen in the mansion.

Winchester Historical Society   Open: June 15-Sept. 15,
225 Prospect St., corner of Lake St.   daily except Sun. & Wed.
Winsted—Phone 379-8433   2-5

The Seymour Inn (1816)

In the delightful rural town of Colebrook, there are a number of interesting, unspoiled early buildings, most of which are privately owned. One of them has been put to practical use, being shared as the Town Hall and the headquarters of the Colebrook Historical Society. This was once the Seymour Inn, built by William Underwood as a wedding present for his daughter, Mrs. Rufus Seymour.

The inn was operated for some time by Mr. and Mrs. Seymour, beginning in 1816, if one accepts the date which appears on the inn's sign, a portion of which is still preserved. Like most of the neighboring dwellings, the house is one of white clapboards, with green blinds; has the characteristic center chimney, and above the front door is a Palladian window.

The historical society has collected many items for its museum, among the outstanding of which are a lap organ, used in the Colebrook Congregational Church from 1799 to 1829; the pewter communion set used in the same church, and manuscript copy of the farewell sermon delivered by its first minister, the Rev. Jonathan Edwards, Jr. Other museum pieces include farm implements, collections of bells, U.S. flags, costumes, uniforms, furniture, pictures, books by Colebrook authors, local historical papers, deeds and diaries, all of which form an interesting background for the history of the community.

Colebrook Historical Society   Open: Memorial Day-
Rts. 182A and 183   Sept., Sat., Sun. &
Colebrook Center—Phone 379-2201   holidays, 2-4 or by
                                                      appointment.

The Dr. Alexander King House (1764)

There are three outstanding features of the Dr. Alexander King Hou' The original long south porch, which has fine feather edge board siding; the exceptionally attractive corner cupboard in the dining room, believed to have been done by Eliphalet King; and the panel painting over the fireplace, attributed to Carlos, son of Dr. Alexander King.

The house is completely furnished with examples from the 17th to 19th century. In the old kitchen is the Thankful Taylor Hadley type chest, dated 1701, and two early Carver type chairs. One of the finest collections of Bennington pottery is on display.

A collection of carriages, wagons and sleighs, and an authentic historic stagecoach are added attractions in their own building. There is also the Cigar Shop where one of the finest collections of cigar-making history is exhibited. The first cigar factory in the United States was established in Suffield in 1810.

Dr. King was a leader in the community, active in all matters pertaining to the welfare of his town, state and country. Much of Dr. King's correspondence with Thomas Jefferson, his close friend, is preserved. He was also one of the members of the State Convention to ratify the U.S. Constitution. Dr. King's diary indicates that he made saltpeter for gunpowder.

Title to the King House remained in the King family until 1869. In 1910 it was purchased by the late Hon. Samuel Reid Spencer. In 1961, Mr. and Mrs. Spencer presented it to the Suffield Historical Society.

Suffield Historical Society   Open: May to November,
234 South Main Street   Wednesdays 2-4
Suffield   50¢

The Hatheway House (1760 & 1795)

Among the many fine colonial homes in Suffield, the Hatheway House on Main Street has been characterized as an outstanding example of "Connecticut Grandeur." Shem Burbank built the main part of the house about 1760 and in 1788 sold it to Oliver Phelps, described as a fabulous land speculator in the "Genesee Country," then a frontier and now a large part of western New York State.

Phelps was lavish in preparing his new home. About 1794, he engaged the best builders in Suffield and Windsor to construct the north wing and apparently moved a small early 18th century building from nearby onto the south side of his house to serve as his land office. Among those working on this new addition was Asher Benjamin, the first native born American architectural author who became a dominant figure in early 19th century building.

The 1795 North Wing is one of the most important parts of the house. It contains one of the few known signed and dated rooms and on its walls are four original French handblocked wallpapers of the 1780's. In addition, this wing contains some of the finest Adamesque plasterwork decoration reflecting the English taste of the 1790's.

Among the architectural details to be observed on the exterior are the block modillions on the main cornice, the molded entablatures with dentils and convex frieze over the windows, the rusticated wooden quoins, and pedimented entrance porch.

By 1802 Phelps had moved to New York State and in 1806 Asahel Hatheway, a wealthy Suffield merchant, bought the house and property.

Antiquarian & Landmarks Society, Inc.
   of Connecticut
Main Street
Suffield—Phone 668-0055

Open: daily May 15 to
October 15, 1-5.
$1.00

The Captain Elisha Phelps House (1771)

Home, tavern, and now museum, the Phelps House has undergone varying changes through the years, yet most of the panelled woodwork remains unchanged. An excellent sampling is found in the North Parlor where the handsomely panelled fireplace wall is surmounted by a row of seven arched glass cupboard doors, with four lights in each. Below are five squares of panelling, and on each side of the fireplace are panels made with witches' crosses. Equally interesting is the second floor ballroom; the original plaster on the unique barrel ceiling is fresh and uncracked.

The Phelps House, a center chimney, gambrel roof structure, built by Captain Elisha Phelps in 1771, has been continuously occupied by members of the family since its construction. After the War of 1812, it was used as a tavern and during the operation of the New Haven and Northampton Canal it was called "The Canal Hotel."

In 1879 the old rear ell was replaced with a new one in the architecture of the Victorian Period. The home was a gift of Mrs. Frederick H. Lovejoy, granddaughter of Jeffry Phelps II, and is a perfect setting for the fine collection of historical objects belonging to the society. Among these are several Higley Coppers, the first copper coinage in America, mined and struck in Simsbury in 1737.

On the grounds surrounding the Phelps House is the Simsbury Historic Center, know as Massacoh Plantation, with buildings of various periods housing items of interest.

The Simsbury Historical Society
800 Hopmeadow Street
Simsbury—Phone 658-2500

Open: daily, May-Oct.
1-4; $1.25, children under
12 and members, free.

The Lieut. Walter Fyler House

Situated in the oldest section of Windsor, in an area dominated by outstanding early dwellings, is the Lieut. Fyler House. While the date of its construction is not definitely known, a portion of it is attributed to Lieut. Walter Fyler, one of Windsor's first settlers, whose home lot in 1640 was at the south end of the land surrounded by palisades, erected for the protection of the families. The home was erected on this site. Fyler served the colony in the Pequot War.

The house was enlarged to its present size when the gambrel roof section was added in the 18th century, probably about 1765. The first floor includes three rooms—a keeping room, an 18th century parlor, and a restored dining room. On the second floor are two small bedrooms and an attic.

After remaining in the possession of the Fyler family for 123 years, the property was acquired in 1763 by Nathaniel Howard, a sea captain, and because of its convenient location, a portion of it was used as a store, and here was established the town's first post office.

The early structure, with its old floors, woodwork and panelling, forms a fine setting for the many possessions of the Windsor Historical Society which has owned the house since 1925.

A splendid museum building has been erected adjacent to the Fyler House.

Windsor Historical Society
96 Palisado Avenue
Windsor—Phone 688-3813

Open: April 1-Dec. 1,
Tues.-Sat. 10-12, 1-4;
50¢, children under 12, 15¢

Oliver Ellsworth Homestead (1740)

Ellsworth Homestead is a fine example of the early central hall house, retaining its original woodwork, framing and panelling. Built on land purchased by Josias Ellsworth in 1665, it remained in the family until 1903, when it was turned over to the Connecticut Daughters of the American Revolution. Oliver Ellsworth, born in 1745, married Abigail Wolcott in 1772 and returned to the homestead about 1780. He constructed the large drawing room and state bedroom.

The house is a fine setting for the lovely pieces of furniture that belonged to the Ellsworth family, among them a Chinese Chippendale sofa with matching chairs, a beautifully carved bedstead, and an exceptional collection of pewter, silver and china. In the bedroom is wallpaper that Ellsworth brought from France about 1800. Downstairs is a photograph of a Gobelin tapestry presented to Ellsworth by Napoleon Bonaparte when he retired as minister plenipotentiary to the Court of France. The tapestry, which once hung in the house, is now on loan to the D.A.R. Museum in Washington, D.C.

Mr. Ellsworth was a member of the Continental Congress, one of the chief framers of the United States Constitution, Senator from Connecticut, third Chief Justice of the United States, and author of the judiciary act forming the basis of the present federal judicial system. He is said to have been George Washington's choice as successor to the presidency. Washington, Lafayette, and President John Adams were all visitors at the homestead.

Connecticut Daughters of the
   American Revolution
778 Palisado Avenue (Rt. 159)
Windsor—Phone 688-9444

Open: May 1-Oct. 31,
Tues.-Sat., 1-6,
donations accepted

Cheney Homestead (c. 1780)

Timothy Cheney, farmer, miller and one of America's famous clock makers, built the Cheney Homestead about 1780. In 1798 George, a son, brought his bride, Electra, to the Homestead to "keep house," and they had nine children. With the exception of George Wells who died, and Seth and John who became well-known artists, all the brothers joined in establishing the Mt. Nebo Silk Company. The firm later became known as Cheney Brothers, world famous in the silk industry.

In the Homestead, the downstairs living room was originally a pine panelled keeping room with massive fireplace and Dutch oven. A tall clock in this room is an example of Timothy's work and is labeled. In the dining room, a later addition once used as a dormitory for the boys, is a set of Chippendale chairs, attributed to Eliphalet Chapin of Windsor. As the Homestead is set into a hillside, the "second floor" is also on ground level with the "front" door of the panelled parlor. Originally a bedroom, the last room to be added to the home has been furnished as a nursery with old pine cradle, spindle crib and a late 19th century dollhouse, all used by Cheney families. Most of the fine 18th century furniture was acquired in Philadelphia by John Cheney, and numerous drawings by Seth, as well as etchings and engravings are to be seen throughout the home.

Manchester Historical Society   Open: Thurs. & Sun. 1-5.
106 Hartford Road   Group tours by app't.
Manchester—Phone 643-5588   50¢, children under 16, free

Mark Twain House (1874)

There are probably very few people acquainted with literature who do not know the work of the famous author, Samuel L. Clemens, or, more popularly, Mark Twain, but there are not so many acquainted with the fact that in 1874 he built a truly remarkable house in Hartford and spent what were the happiest years of his life residing there. Designed by Edward T. Potter of New York, to comply with the whims of the author, this large, rambling structure has no counterpart elsewhere.

It is built with red brick, with orange and black painted bands for ornamentation, studded with elaborate porches, balconies, gables and chimneys, while the interior is equally unmatched with rooms of unusual design, mahogany doors and woodwork with silver stencil designed by Tiffany. Some of the Clemens furniture is still on display. The formal parlor has its original chandelier and pier glass. The library was the family living room, where its original mantelpiece has been returned and restored, and in the dining room is the large window over the fireplace, where Mark Twain "could watch the flames leaping to meet the falling snow flakes." Displayed also is a Paige typesetting machine and a highwheeled bicycle belonging to him, and original drawings for his books.

The house saw a constant flow of guests, and few who had entree failed to stop when in the vicinity. Letters from these praise the elegance of the quarters, the lavish entertainment and the warm scintillating atmosphere in which the Clemens family life abounded. Restoration of the house has brought back this feeling of an era of grandeur and vivacity.

Mark Twain Memorial
351 Farmington Avenue
Hartford—Phone 247-0998

Open: hours vary according
to season, call before
visiting.

Harriet Beecher Stowe House (1871)

One of the most famous books written in the 19th century was "Uncle Tom's Cabin." Its author, Harriet Beecher Stowe, lived in this modest, brick Gothic style house on Forest Street in Hartford from 1873 to 1896. Just across the lawn on Farmington Avenue was the home of Mark Twain. Together these two individuals helped to make up an unusual literary community known then (and now) as Nook Farm.

The Stowe house has been carefully restored through the use of documents and photographs so that it looks as nearly as possible as it did when Mrs. Stowe lived there. Besides the reproduction of such things as the diamond pattern wallpaper for the front hall, and the Wilton carpeting for the front and rear parlors, there are many paintings and pieces of furniture which belonged to Mrs. Stowe. The Victorian grace of the home is enhanced through the use of many plants and flower arrangements. In fact, Mrs. Stowe wrote a book, "The American Woman's Home" in which she suggested many uses for plants in decorating a home. Many of Mrs. Stowe's own paintings in the house depict wild flowers and bouquets, giving further proof of her love of nature.

Although Mrs. Stowe was in her early 60's when she lived in this house, she was still actively writing. She wrote in the small study off her bedroom on the second floor. Other delightful features of this house are the restored bathroom and kitchen which display many of the "latest" facilities and utensils of the late nineteenth century.

Harriet Beecher Stowe House
73 Forest Street
Hartford—Phone 525-9317

Open: hours and admissions
same as Mark Twain
Memorial.

The Butler-McCook Homestead (1782)

Since 1782 the Butler-McCook Homestead, a rare historic survivor in an ever changing urban area, has stood (at 396) on Main Street in Hartford.

As it stands today, the Homestead is the result of an architectural evolution reflecting the four generations who continuously occupied the building until 1971. This evolution is evident in the panelled fireplace walls which were "modernized" in the 1860's with marble mantels and in the dormers added to accommodate a growing family.

Nowhere is the reflection of changing taste more obvious than in the wide variety of furnishings, all of which were found in the Homestead. Fine examples of 18th century furniture seen in Windsor chairs, a cherry Queen Anne Period secretary-desk, a matching highboy and lowboy, side by side with Empire and Victorian Period pieces. In addition, there are interesting individual collections of Japanese armor, Chinese bronzes, Egyptian statuettes, American silver, 19th century toys and dolls, and late 18th and mid 19th century American paintings.

At the rear of the property the 1866 carriage house now contains a museum of old family bikes, sleds, military uniforms and sports equipment.

Of special interest is the garden which has been restored to the mid 19th century period following the original plan found in the Homestead. This rare surviving drawing is by Jacob Weidenman, landscape architect, and is dated 1865. The garden and expansive lawn create a unique oasis and quiet reminder of by-gone days in the midst of a growing modern city.

Antiquarian & Landmarks Society, Inc.   Open: May 15 to
   of Connecticut   Oct. 15, 1-5
394 Main Street $1.00
Hartford—Phone 247-8996

Noah Webster

Literally millions of our forebears of the nineteenth century studied from Webster's Speller and Grammar, among the first American schoolbooks. The "American" dictionary that is consulted today is based, to a large degree, on Webster's original dictionary. In the course of his 85 years, Webster worked as a schoolteacher, lawyer, editor, lecturer, writer, judge and legislator. He wrote extensively on many subjects, including disease, science, history, and the importance of national unity.

The Noah Webster House is an excellent example of a typical 18th century Connecticut farmhouse. Noah, one of five Webster children, was born here in the "West Division" of Hartford in 1758. Noah's father was a farmer and worked the land of about 120 acres with his sons. Noah left the farm at the age of 16 to attend Yale, but after graduation, returned to the homestead while he taught school in Hartford and West Hartford.

The house is typical of the time, with a central chimney, and an added lean-to at the rear, making a total of seven rooms. In the kitchen is an unusually large (9 ft.) fireplace with two bake ovens, one of which is original. The north parlor and north chamber retain their fine original panelling, and the floor boards and the stairporch on the second floor are also original. The Noah Webster House is modestly furnished in the period of the 18th century, and has a recreated 18th century garden. At announced times there are cooking and spinning demonstrations at the house.

Noah Webster Foundation &
  Historical Society
227 South Main Street
West Hartford—Phone 521-1939

Open: Thurs. 10-4,
Sun. 2-4. Other times
by appointment.
50¢, children 25¢

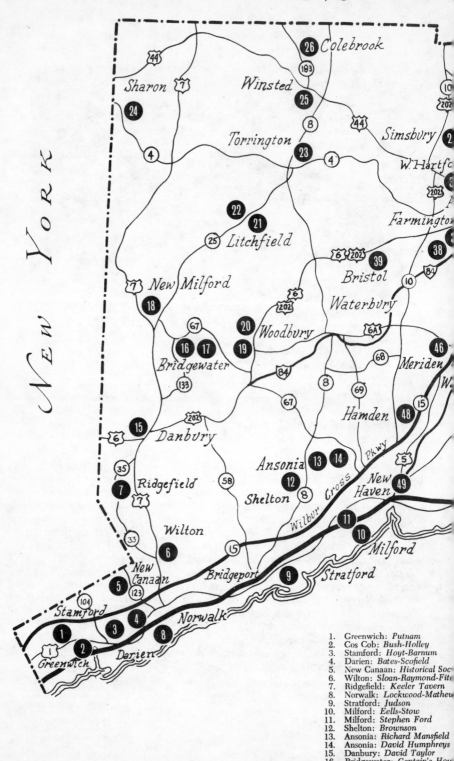

MASS.

New York

26 Colebrook
44
183
Sharon
7
24
Winsted
25
4
Torrington
8
23 44
4
Simsbury
10 202
W. Hartfc
202
22
21
25 Litchfield
6 202
39 38
7 New Milford
6
202
Bristol
Waterbury
18
67
20 Woodbury
6A
16 17 19
68 Meriden
Bridgewater
84
46
133
8 69
202
15
67
48 15
Danbury
Hamden
35
Ansonia
13 14 5
7 Ridgefield
58
12
New 49
7
Shelton
8 Haven
33
Wilton
11
Wilbur Cross Pkwy
10 Milford
6
15
New
Bridgeport
9 Stratford
5 Canaan
104 123
1 Stamford
3 4 Norwalk
2
8
Greenwich
Darien

1. Greenwich: *Putnam*
2. Cos Cob: *Bush-Holley*
3. Stamford: *Hoyt-Barnum*
4. Darien: *Bates-Scofield*
5. New Canaan: *Historical Soc*
6. Wilton: *Sloan-Raymond-Fite*
7. Ridgefield: *Keeler Tavern*
8. Norwalk: *Lockwood-Matheu*
9. Stratford: *Judson*
10. Milford: *Eells-Stow*
11. Milford: *Stephen Ford*
12. Shelton: *Brownson*
13. Ansonia: *Richard Mansfield*
14. Ansonia: *David Humphreys*
15. Danbury: *David Taylor*
16. Bridgewater: *Captain's Hou*
17. Bridgewater: *Elijah Peck*
18. New Milford: *Historical Soc*

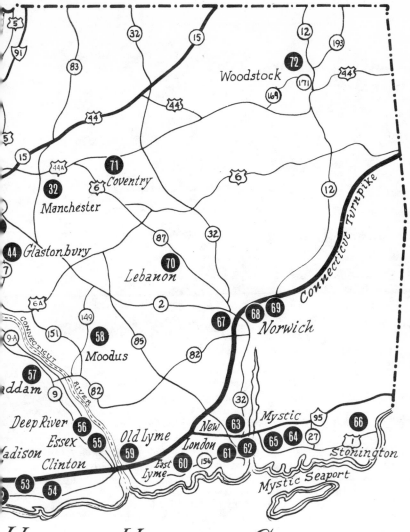

HISTORIC HOUSES OF CONNECTICUT
Open to the public

Woodbury: *Glebe*	37. Farmington: *Stanley-Whitman*	55. Essex: *Lt. Wm. Pratt*
Woodbury: *Hurd*	38. Farmington: *Hill-Stead*	56. Deep River: *Stone House*
Litchfield: *Tapping Reeve*	39. Bristol: *Miles Lewis*	57. Haddam: *Thankful Arnold*
Litchfield: *Deacon Peter Buell*	40. Wethersfield: *Buttolph-Williams*	58. Moodus: *Amasa Day*
Torrington: *Hotchkiss-Fyler*	41. Wethersfield: *Joseph Webb*	59. Old Lyme: *Florence Griswold*
Sharon: *Gay-Hoyt*	42. Wethersfield: *Isaac Stevens*	60. East Lyme: *Thomas Lee*
Winsted: *Solomon Rockwell*	43. Wethersfield: *Silas Deane*	61. New London: *Hempsted*
Colebrook: *Seymour Inn*	44. S. Glastonbury: *Welles-Shipman-Ward*	62. New London: *Shaw*
Suffield: *Hatheway*	45. Middletown: *General Mansfield*	63. New London: *Deshon-Allyn*
Suffield: *Dr. Alexander King*	46. Meriden: *Andrews*	64. Mystic: *Denison*
Simsbury: *Elisha Phelps*	47. Wallingford: *Parsons*	65. Mystic: *Buckingham*
Windsor: *Lt. Walter Fyler*	48. Hamden: *Jonathan Dickerman*	66. Stonington: *Whitehall*
Windsor: *Oliver Ellsworth*	49. New Haven: *Morris*	67. Norwich: *Leffingwell Inn*
Manchester: *Cheney*	50. Guilford: *Henry Whitfield*	68. Norwich: *Rockwell*
Hartford: *Mark Twain*	51. Guilford: *Hyland*	69. Norwich: *Nathaniel Backus*
Hartford: *Harriet Beecher Stowe*	52. Guilford: *Thomas Griswold*	70. Lebanon: *Gov. Jonathan Trumbull*
Hartford: *Butler-McCook*	53. Madison: *Nathaniel Allis*	71. Coventry: *Hale Homestead*
W. Hartford: *Noah Webster*	54. Clinton: *Adam Stanton*	72. Woodstock: *Henry C. Bowen*

Stanley-Whitman House (c. 1660)

There is probably no finer example of a 17th century dwelling to be found in New England than the Stanley-Whitman House, a Registered National Historic Landmark. While the exact date of its construction is not known, its distinctive architectural features, according to authorities, indicate that it was built about 1660.

The great center chimney of stone and the framed overhang reflect a distinct survival of Elizabethan or Jacobean architecture, brought from England by the first settlers. The drops, or pendants, below the wide overhang of the second story, add a rare touch of ornamentation.

In 1935 the owners of the house, Mr. and Mrs. D. Newton Barney had the house restored under the direction of J. Frederick Kelly, and deeded the property to the Village Green and Library Association.

Opposite the front entrance, the stairway, built against the center chimney, leads to the second floor, while on either side is the parlor and hall, each with a large fireplace of original masonry. Beyond is the "lean to" with kitchen, buttery and "birth and death" room, probably added about 1760. The house is completely furnished with rare pieces of early American design, many of them gifts of local residents.

Among the pieces are several fashioned by local cabinetmakers, or the work of other Connecticut artisans, including clocks, chests, chairs, tables, highboys, desks, and a lamp collection.

A fireproof wing houses exhibits of old manuscripts, glass, china, silver, pewter, musical instruments and other items associated with historic Farmington.

Farmington Museum   Open: Sun. 2-5; Apr. 1-Nov. 30,
High Street   weekdays except Mon., 10-12,
Farmington—Phone 677-9222   2-5; Dec. 1-Mar. 31, Fri. & Sat.,
                                                     10-12, 2-5. $1.00

Hill-Stead Museum (1900)

In sharp contrast to the architecture and furnishings of the Farmington Museum, scarcely two blocks away, Hill-Stead Museum represents the utmost in design and accessories of a beautiful mansion, erected at the beginning of the twentieth century. Architecturally reminiscent of Mount Vernon, it was built for Mr. and Mrs. Alfred Atmore Pope, and was designed by their daughter, Theodate, and the famous architect, Stanford White.

Miss Pope, who later became the wife of John Wallace Riddle, former American representative to Russia, Turkey and Argentina, also designed and built Avon Old Farms, a school for boys, near Farmington.

Mr. Pope, a wealthy steel magnate, made a remarkable collection of paintings of the Impressionist School, when many of the artists were but little known in this country, and used his 29-room home for displaying his collections. Exquisitely furnished, the house was left by Mrs. Riddle to a private trust, to be maintained as Hill-Stead Museum, just as it was lived in at the time of her death in 1946.

Displayed are paintings by Manet, Monet, Degas, Mary Cassatt, Whistler and others, while the lovely furnishings include fine old period pieces, glass, china, prints and etchings, and many fascinating objects of art collected from all parts of the world. The library contains a great variety of old and modern books on many subjects.

Hill-Stead Museum   Open: Wed., Thurs., Sat.
Mountain Rd. & Farmington Ave.   & Sun., 2-5.
Farmington—Phone 677-9064   50¢, children 25¢

Miles Lewis House (1801)

Situated in the heart of what was once the center of the clock-making industry of the country, the Miles Lewis House, erected in 1801, is now the home of the American Clock and Watch Museum, the only museum devoted exclusively to the History of American Horology.

It is an excellent example of the mansion house of the post-revolutionary period, and with the exception of a new staircase, remains as it was erected by Lewis. The great halls on each floor are flanked on either side with twin rooms, and on the first floor is the spacious ell kitchen. Chestnut and oak were used in its construction, while the flooring was of swamp maple. In keeping with its period, the house is furnished with many attractive pieces, including some attributed to clock makers, which give it the appearance of its earlier days.

The outstanding feature of the house is the unexcelled collection of clocks and watches, representing every type imaginable, produced by the early craftsmen of America. Each item is carefully labeled, giving its date and manufacturer, and in addition to the great array of timepieces, the tools of the craft are also exhibited. For those interested in research, there is a splendid library.

At the rear of the house, occupying the site of the original kitchen garden, is the Ebenezer Barnes Wing containing the curator's office, fireproof library vault, repair and storage facilities. Although it is a modern building, this wing has interior construction and panelling from the Ebenezer Barnes home, the first permanent residence built in Bristol, c. 1728.

American Clock & Watch
  Museum, Inc.
100 Maple Street
Bristol

Open: daily, except Mon.,
April-Oct., 1-5. Groups
by appointment.

Buttolph-Williams House (1692)

There is hardly a dwelling more characteristic of late 17th century architecture than the one built by David Buttolph. He lived in the house a very short time, and by 1711, it had become the property of Benjamin Beldon, who was licensed to keep a tavern. It was sold to Daniel Williams in 1721, who occupied it with his family for many years. By 1947, the house had become the property of the Antiquarian & Landmarks Society of Connecticut. During restoration, many fascinating discoveries were made, one of which was finding the original riven oak clapboards beneath the relatively modern clapboards. Today the house has very much the same appearance as it had when constructed.

Here is assembled an outstanding collection of very early American antiques. "Ye Greate Kitchin," with its many utensils, tables, chairs and benches, wooden ware, pewter and other accessories, is the most completely furnished room of its kind in New England. Elsewhere are many other rare items—a unique 17th century fireback, oak and pine Hartford chest, mushroom armchairs, early delft, court cupboards, and homespun linen. An early Buttolph inventory enumerates thirty trenchers, the number now in the house, together with a jack and weights for turning the spit before the fireplace. Also treasured is the rare 17th century half circle settle, as is the trestle-foot gateleg table, together with the rare twin high chairs. This house is a Registered National Historic Landmark.

Antiquarian & Landmarks
  Society, Inc. of Connecticut
Broad Street
Wethersfield—Phone 529-0460

Open: daily 1-5, May 15 to
Oct. 15
50¢

Joseph Webb House (1752)

Few houses in the country have greater historical significance than the Joseph Webb House. It was here in May 1781 that General Washington spent five days in conference with Count de Rochambeau, making campaign plans for the American and French troops, which ultimately led to the Battle of Yorktown and the establishment of American independence. Arrangements for the conference were made by Samuel Webb, who was Washington's private secretary and a brother of Joseph Webb, Jr.

The main portion of the house was constructed by Joseph Webb, Sr. in 1752. Its gambrel roof, brownstone underpinnings, columnar front entrance porch, central hall, Georgian staircase and fine panelling about the fireplace contribute to its architectural distinction. In 1961 the house was designated as a National Historical Landmark.

Many important political figures, including Governor Jonathan Trumbull, Colonel Jeremiah Wadsworth, General Henry Knox and other visiting dignitaries were entertained here, giving it the name of "Hospitality Hall." The room where Washington slept still retains its original imported wallpaper and is authentically furnished, as are all of the other rooms, displaying the outstanding taste and meticulous workmanship of the early cabinetmakers. Chinese export porcelain, lovely English silver, early crewel work and tapestries, and many other authentic and rare items show 18th century living at its best.

National Society of The Colonial
  Dames of America in the State
  of Connecticut
211 Main Street
Wethersfield—Phone 529-0612

Open: Tues.-Sat. 10-4,
Sun. 1-4, mid-May to
mid-Oct. $1.00.
Tour of 3 houses $2.50.
Children and groups less.

Isaac Stevens House (1788-9)

In marked contrast to the formal elegance of its next door neighbor, the Webb House, the Isaac Stevens House is more simple in character, a plain, but substantial and well-proportioned country home. Built in 1788-9 by Stevens for his bride, the dwelling remained in the same family for a period of 170 years, when it was acquired by the Connecticut Society of Colonial Dames of America, to insure its preservation in this historic town.

Of peaked roof construction, with a beautiful crown molding, its exterior has a unique and original feature, the rear being enclosed with weatherboarding instead of the usual clapboards. At the door yard is a well and a small herb garden, once an important adjunct to the early homes. As it was no longer considered authentic because of many alterations, an ell that was added to the house perhaps some six to ten years after the original construction, has been removed.

The interior is planned with a central hall, with four rooms on the first floor and five bedrooms on the second. Its early panelling, kitchen fireplace, original hand-fashioned hardware and other features remain, including the sliding blinds, or "Indian shutters," at the first floor windows. There are still the original lights over the back door, which retains its early paint.

On display are many possessions of the Stevens family, including furniture, glass, china and cooking utensils, but especially noteworthy is the fact that it has an emphasis on children, with a small museum containing toys, books, clothes and other items relating to members of the younger generation.

National Society of The Colonial
   Dames of America in the State
   of Connecticut
215 Main Street
Wethersfield—Phone 529-0612

Open: see Webb House
for details

Silas Deane House (1766)

Silas Deane, the controversial patriot, planned and built this house in its entirety after he married Mehitabel, widow of Joseph Webb, whose famous house stands next door. Deane was an ambitious, clever man whose fortunes were on the rise and this house reflects his dramatic originality. Here plans were laid for the capture of Fort Ticonderoga and here George Washington was entertained en route to assume command of the Continental Army in Cambridge.

But Deane's star set almost at its zenith. While he was serving as minister plenipotentiary from the Continental Congress to the Court of Louis XVI in France, a rival accused him of speculation in the purchase of war supplies for the Continental Armies. He was recalled to Philadelphia to report his activities, was denied a full hearing, but was promised an audit which was never made. He finally returned to France, bitter and impoverished, where he wrote ill-advised letters, also used against him. He died in exile and poverty in England. In 1842, Deane's heirs were awarded $37,000 by Congress with a final judgment that Silas Deane had not been a traitor.

The rooms of this mansion are of graceful proportions. In the living room is a fireplace of carved Connecticut brownstone; the dining room and library are richly panelled; the kitchen boasts an enormous fireplace. Plans include the restoration of the unusual front piazza. This unique house was made a National Historic Landmark in 1973.

National Society of The Colonial
   Dames of America in the State
   of Connecticut
203 Main Street
Wethersfield—Phone 529-0612

Open: see Webb House
for details

The Welles-Shipman-Ward House (1755)

This outstanding example of mid 18th century Connecticut River Valley architecture is owned and maintained by The Historical Society of Glastonbury. A two-story, center chimney house, the Welles-Shipman-Ward House received a citation from the Department of the Interior "as possessing exceptional architectural interest" and "as being worthy of the most careful preservation."

John Welles, the original owner, was a descendant of Thomas Welles, the early colonial governor who helped write the Fundamental Orders of Connecticut. He operated a shipyard in South Glastonbury and generously supported the Revolution with his time, effort and business resources. Stephen Shipman, Jr. acquired the house in 1789-90 and the property remained in the Shipman family for many years. Dr. and Mrs. James Ward bought it in 1925 and started restoration.

Original documents reveal the room designations. In the southwest room there is an elegant corner cupboard, crown molding broken with slight offsets on the encased summer beam and panelled fireplace wall. The northwest room has sliding interior shutters, a wide panel and fluted pilasters on the fireplace wall and panelled wainscoting. There is an impressive fireplace in the kitchen with two ovens in the rear wall.

The Historical Society of Glastonbury also opens its headquarters, the Town Hall Museum to the public on Sundays, 2-4, April 15 through October 15. Built ca. 1837, it is located on Main Street next to the Green Cemetery, the oldest burial ground in Glastonbury.

The Historical Society
  of Glastonbury, Inc.
972 Main Street, Route 17
South Glastonbury

Open: Sundays, 2-4
June through September.
Small admission fee.

The General Mansfield House (1810)

None of Connecticut's open houses has a closer association with the Civil War period than the General Joseph King Fenno Mansfield House, for it was here that this Regular Army officer made his home for a number of years. Construction of this brick town house was commenced in 1807 by Robert Robinson for Samuel and Catherine Livingston Mather and was completed in 1810. About the turn of the century, alterations were made to the interior and a wing to the north and west was added.

In 1838 the Mather's daughter, Louisa Maria, and Mansfield were married and, except for a brief period, this was their home through the balance of their lives. A graduate of the U.S. Military Academy, Mansfield was a member of the Corps of Engineers and for a time was Inspector General of the Army. He saw service in the Mexican War and spent considerable time on the then frontier sections of the country. He commanded troops at the battle of Antietam, where he was mortally wounded, September 17, 1862. He died the following day and his body was returned to Middletown for interment.

Items relating to the General's life are in the possession of the Society, as well as letters from important personages, fine pieces of furniture, a chair used by George Washington, a Harland grandfather clock, and other material that is worthy of note.

Middlesex County Historical Society   Open: Wednesdays 3-5
151 Main Street   and by appointment.
Middletown—Phone 346-0746   35¢

The Andrews Homestead (1760)

Almost at the edge of the business center of Meriden there has fortunately been preserved a fine colonial dwelling of excellent architectural form, typical of the Connecticut saltbox, with two lean-tos at the back. This is the Andrews Homestead, possibly constructed in 1760 by its first owner, Moses Andrews, members of his family having been known to be carpenters. Moses built the house on the edge of his father's farm, the latter having taken up land in that area many years earlier.

Notwithstanding its numerous changes in ownership and the various uses to which it has been put, its characteristic features remain—the massive center chimney, fireplaces, fine panelling, delicately turned bannisters and other details.

Moses Andrews is best known for his activities in behalf of the Episcopal Church. Like many others of his religious faith, he came under suspicion during the Revolutionary War days and was ordered confined to his own property. Denied permission to attend Sunday services, he invited his neighbors to congregate at his home, and from this developed a formal organization of the church Society in 1789.

The Homestead is now owned by the City, but is leased to the Meriden Historical Society, which maintains it as a museum. It is attractively furnished and displays many items of interest—early chests, bedsteads, tables, clocks, tableware and numerous "made in Meriden" products.

Meriden Historical Society   Open: Wed. & Sun. 2-5, when
424 West Main Street   resident custodian is at home, or
Meriden—Phone 237-5079   by appointment.
                                      $1.00, children free.

Parsons House (1759)

Once a tavern and stopping point for stagecoaches plying between New York and Boston, the attractive colonial red, gambrel roof dwelling, now the home of the Wallingford Historical Society, was built for Samuel Parsons in 1759, and in 1855 a small ell was added. Except for recent structural improvements, few changes have been made in this house, located not too far from the stockades built in 1676 for the protection of the early settlers.

The Parsons family occupied the house until 1803, when it was deeded to Captain Caleb Thompson. This family retained it until 1919 when Mrs. Fannie Ives Schember, granddaughter of Captain Caleb Thompson, bequeathed it to the society, which had been founded in 1916.

Six fireplaces, together with interesting cupboards, good panelling, chair rails and other woodwork provide an authentic background for the many items to be found here. Two period rooms of the 18th and 19th centuries have been carefully arranged and furnished. There is a library of many old volumes and documents; a pantry with old china; one room entirely devoted to Civil War relics; another to small farm tools, and still another to firearms. A large showcase in the museum room exhibits linen, costumes, silver, pewter, musical instruments, school books, Indian pieces and old coins.

The attic features a large loom and a genealogical chart of the Hall family, dating from 1605. A descendant, Lyman Hall, one of the signers of the Declaration of Independence, was born in Wallingford.

Wallingford Historical Society   Open: Sundays 2-5, other
180 South Main Street   days by appointment.
Wallingford—Phone 269-6257

Jonathan Dickerman "Old Red House"

A simple, red, story and a half house, with center chimney and a roof sweep which extends over its front, was erected almost in the shadow of Hamden's famed "Sleeping Giant," and was originally the home of Jonathan Dickerman II. He undoubtedly built the house about 1770, the year he married Miriam Bradley. The ceremony was performed by the Rev. Nathaniel Sherman. Jonathan was one of nineteen children, born in his father's home nearby.

The house, which at an earlier date had two ells, but since removed, was associated with the Dickerman family through an entire century. Amelia and Philas Dickerman owned it for many years and during the 1850's it was the home of Caroline A. Dickerman, a great-granddaughter of the builder. Early in the twentieth century it was bought by Homer B. Tuttle, who married Augusta E. Dickerman, the great great granddaughter of Jonathan II. Mr. Tuttle sold the house to John Edward Heaton and it was from him that the Sleeping Giant Park Association received it as a gift in 1924.

The Hamden Historical Society, organized in 1928, has maintained the house and opened it to the public as an historic site.

The Connecticut State Park and Forest Commission, through legislative action, transferred the old house to the Hamden Historical Society in June, 1961.

The Hamden Historical Society
Mt. Carmel Avenue
Mt. Carmel—248-7064/248-0809

Open: Sat. and Sun. 2-5,
mid May to mid Oct., and
by appointment.

Morris House (1685-1779)

While New Haven's historic Green, laid out about the time of the settlement of the town in 1638, survives, very few of its early houses still remain. Among these, however, is the Morris House. The first dwelling on the site was erected by Eleazar Morris in 1685. A massive stone end, incorporating the chimney and fireplaces, formed its north wall.

Detailed study has led to some fascinating theories regarding the enlargement of the house, for as the Morris family grew, rooms were added and another wall of masonry was constructed at the south, while an ell became the "new" kitchen. On July 5, 1779, British troops landed nearby, and on their march toward New Haven, this mansion was burned.

As the foundations and stone walls survived the fire, Amos Morris, the owner at that time, immediately started the reconstruction of the house, although it took a period of nearly ten years to complete it. Further changes were made during the 19th century, including the installation of a second story ballroom.

The house was purchased in 1915 by William S. Pardee, who did some restoration work, and in 1918 he bequeathed it to the New Haven Colony Historical Society. Under the ownership of this organization further restorations have been made. Furnished appropriately, it is now the sole surviving structure of its period in New Haven still retaining most of its character.

New Haven Colony Historical Society
325 Lighthouse Road (via Townsend
   Ave. from Exit 50, Conn. Tnpk.)
New Haven—Phone 467-0764

Open: May 1 to Nov. 1,
weekdays 10-5, Sundays 2-5.
Closed Saturday.

Henry Whitfield House (1639)

The Rev. Henry Whitfield, founder of the town of Guilford, leader of one of the earliest groups of colonists in the United States, and an important figure in the religious world of his day, built what is probably the oldest stone house in the country, at about the time of the settlement in 1639. Having come from England, the builder erected what was a representative example of an elaborate English Midlands manor house of the 16th-17th centuries, with steeply pitched roof, small windows, and great hall.

The Great Hall is thirty-three feet long and fifteen feet wide, with a huge fireplace at each end. In the middle of it is a partition hinged to a second floor joist, which either divides the room into two or swings up to the ceiling out of the way. The only other room on the first floor is the kitchen.

In its early days the house served not only as a dwelling place for Whitfield, his wife Dorothy, and seven of their nine children, but also as a headquarters for the community of twenty-five families, and as a garrison and meeting house. During its history the house served various purposes, was gutted by fire in 1865, rebuilt in 1868, and in 1902 it became a museum owned by the state. Just prior to 1939, the house was restored, as far as it is known, to its original form by the architect, J. Frederick Kelly. About a third of the present building is original.

As a museum, there are on display rare and authentic pieces of 17th century household furnishings of all descriptions: exhibits of early weaving, metal working and crafts, a contemporary herb garden, and many unusual items.

State of Connecticut
Whitfield St., ½ mile S. of Exit
58, Interstate 95
Guilford—Phone 453-2457

Open: Jan. 15-Dec. 15 except
Mon. & Tues. Apr.-Oct. 11-5,
Nov.-Mar. 11-4. 50¢, children
under 12, free.

The Hyland House (1600)

A fine example of an early saltbox, with added lean-to, was built by George Hyland about 1660. Original, unpainted clapboards, still to be seen in the keeping room, attest to the fact that the lean-to was probably annexed in 1720 when Ebenezer Parmelee acquired the house. Another unique feature is the chamferred overhang on the sides of the main house—a refinement marking it as one of the finer houses of its day.

Here one has the feeling of visiting a 17th century family, for the house is completely furnished with authentic appointments of the period—the Bible box, complete array of kitchen utensils around the fireplace, a loom ready to use, the Guilford chest with its original painted decoration. An early chairtable, a Carver chair, tavern tables and other interesting pieces of furniture are in place. A pencil post bed covered with a resist-dyed quilt, is in one of the chambers.

Here, too, one finds an original window casement, some fascinating old panelling, as well as the butterfly and H and HL hinges which are part of the original hardware. The staircase leading to the second floor is handsome, and the same fine work is lavished equally on the stairway to the attic.

In this house Ebenezer Parmelee made the first town clock in America, completed in 1726, for the steeple of the Congregational Church.

Dorothy Whitfield Historical Society   Open: June 25-Sept. 9,
84 Boston Street   daily except Monday,
Guilford   10:30-4:30. 50¢

Thomas Griswold House (1735)

"A saltbox of exquisite proportions" is the term used by Samuel Chamberlain, noted photographer, in tersely and accurately describing the Thomas Griswold House. From its construction in 1735, the dwelling remained the property of the Griswold family until 1958, when it was purchased by the Guilford Keeping Society.

Standing on a slight rise of ground above the road and separated from the highway by a fence which once served as part of the ornamentation of the belfry of the First Congregational Church, which stood on the Green prior to 1828, the house presents a pleasing picture of antiquity. In fact, its beauty was so recognized that its picture once appeared on a commemorative stamp.

The purpose of the Keeping Society is to preserve the best of "old" Guilford—its architecture, history, records and legends, with the result that one may find here many exceptional items of the town's artifacts from 1735 to the present day, rather than a furnished house of any particular period. However, early wallpaper, harmonizing with old paint tones, helps to accentuate the numerous fine pieces of furniture.

The house serves the community for meetings, special exhibits and similar purposes. At the rear of the house, the village blacksmith building houses an old ox sling.

Guilford Keeping Society
171 Boston Street
Guilford—Phone 453-3176

Open: daily except Mon.
& Tues., 11-5; closed
Dec. 1-Mar. 31.
50¢, children under 12 free

Nathaniel Allis House (c. 1785)

Madison was one of Connecticut's early towns, and in this community where fine colonial homes survive, the Nathaniel Allis House is one of the landmarks. Built around 1785 by Aaron Blatchley, the house was originally a one-story building of four rooms. Later a second story was built and extra rooms added in the back. In the 1860's the house was extended eastward, providing several more rooms.

Two generations of the Allis family lived here, following which it was owned briefly by Ichabod Lee Scranton in 1825, and who in the same year sold it to Nathan Bushnell. Nathan was the father of Cornelius S. Bushnell, who was born in the house and who became one of the promoters of the "Shore Line" Railroad, a shipbuilder who provided many vessels for the government, and who largely financed with his own funds, the construction of the "Monitor," the definitive ironclad of the Civil War.

The four corner fireplaces, heavy beams, corner posts, fine original panelling, and other interior details provide a splendid setting for the lovely furnishings and numerous items which are on display.

A large carriage house and a corn crib just beyond the dwelling provide additional space for exhibits, including early farm tools, household utensils, looms, Indian artifacts, Civil War relics and many items of local historic interest.

Madison Historical Society
853 Boston Post Road
Madison—Phone 245-4567

Open: June 15-Sept. 15,
daily 10-5 except Sun. & Mon.
50¢, children under 12 free

Adam Stanton House (c. 1790)

The Adam Stanton House was built between 1789 and 1791 on the site of an earlier house. The Rev. Abraham Pierson, whose house originally occupied the property, was the first rector, or president, of Yale College. Adam Stanton had opened a retail store in 1777, and in 1804 moved the business into the east ell which he had built for that purpose. The store operated until 1864.

Three generations of Stantons lived in this fine old house and the last of the family, Lewis Elliot Stanton, left it as a public museum in memory of his brother, John Adam Stanton, who had gathered 18th and 19th century furnishings appropriate for the house. These included ancestral pieces, gateleg tables, high post beds, china and pewter, and embroideries in silk made by the family. Even the two attics possess many interesting and unusual items.

A unique feature of the house is the fact that the wooden partitions between the two front rooms and the front hall were hung on H and L hinges in order that the partitions could be swung upward, hooked to the ceiling, and the front of the house thus thrown into one room for assemblies, dances and other social gatherings.

Of special interest is the replica of a country store which occupies the ell of the building.

Hartford National Bank
63 E. Main Street
Clinton—Phone 669-2132

Open: May 1-Nov. 1, daily
except Mon., afternoons till
5; July & Aug. 11-5; winter
by appointment

Lt. William Pratt House

Essex is one of the loveliest coastal towns in New England. Among its earliest settlers was Lt. William Pratt, who had gone with the Rev. Thomas Hooker and his group from Massachusetts to Hartford in 1636, and then, in 1645 had migrated to Saybrook, parent town of Essex. Here he built a small, one-room dwelling, which he enlarged to a four-room gambrel roofed house. He served in the Pequot War, was made a lieutenant in 1661, and from 1666 until his death in 1678, he was a representative in the General Court.

The main portion of the structure was probably erected c. 1678. It was bequeathed by Mr. and Mrs. Samuel Griswold in 1952 to the Society for the Preservation of New England Antiquities, and since its restoration has been outstanding as a museum, representative of its period. The center chimney, fireplaces, the beaded pine sheathing, hand hewn oak and chestnut beams, the gunstock corner posts, wide floor boards and other details are features of its construction.

Among the furnishings are a collection of courting mirrors, pewter made by Joseph Danforth of Middletown, a cherry chest-on-chest, maple tester bed, mahogany lowboy, mahogany highboy with scroll top attributed to Elijah Booth of Woodbury, and other fine pieces of early craftsmen.

Society for the Preservation of   Open: June 1-Oct. 31,
    New England Antiquities   Tues., Thurs. & Sat. 1-5,
20 West Avenue   50¢, children free.
Essex—Phone 767-1003

The Stone House (1840)

Representative of one of the important early industries of the lower Connecticut River Valley, that of quarrying building stone, the present headquarters of the Deep River Historical Society was erected in 1840 for Deacon Ezra Southworth and his bride, Eunice Post. The Southworth family was an important one and the Stone House remained in possession of the family until it was bequeathed to the Historical Society by Ada Southworth Munson in 1947. Deep River was at one time a portion of the original town of Saybrook.

The original house had a flat tin roof, with slight slope to the back. Later a plain hip roof was constructed over the first, which then became the present attic floor. Other Victorian changes made in the 1880's included the addition of a large gable and the building of a pillared porch, together with a wood ell on the rear. The latter was rebuilt in the 1950's to suit the convenience of the society. The barn was also remodeled to conform to the house.

Of special interest today is the Marine Room which contains many items relating to local Connecticut River history. There are over 100 pieces of cut glass made in Deep River, and also on display is a group of oil paintings of the 1840-50 period by a local artist, O. Dickinson.

Deep River Historical Society
South Main Street
Deep River—Phone 526-2609

Open: Thurs. afternoons in summer; other times by appointment with curator, Mrs. Donald R. Moore.

Thankful Arnold House (c. 1795-1870)

One of the homes most recently restored to museum standards, the Thankful Arnold House is a charming example of a medium-sized family house of the late 18th, early 19th century. Its lovely setting is the picturesque Haddam town green.

The oldest portion was built about 1794-1795 by Joseph Arnold (1773-1823), a direct descendant and namesake of one of Haddam's 28 founders. The second phase came in 1798-1800 to accommodate Joseph and his wife Thankful, who he had married in January, 1796. She was the daughter of Joseph and Sarah Dudley Clark of Chester, and was a direct descendant of Priscilla and John Alden of Plymouth. The young Arnolds proceeded to have thirteen children, born 1797 through 1822. One of these was Samuel Arnold (1806-1869), Haddam's U.S. Congressman from 1857 to 1859. Another child was Isaac Arnold (1815-1892), the great-grandfather of Isaac Arnold of Houston, Texas, who, with his wife Agnes Cullen Arnold, has generously restored the house. The third phase of the house involved moving an older structure to join the first two sections sometime before 1810.

The fabric of the house has been completely restored and boasts some lovely simple panelling. Presently it is being furnished with suitable period pieces. One hall passageway has been decorated with wall stencilling copied from the Selden House (c. 1800) of Haddam Neck and is furnished with examples from the same house. There are pieces on loan from other Haddam houses and several decorative items have been in the house at least since the inventory of 1823. A period garden is in plans for the future.

Haddam Historical Society, Inc.   Open: June 1-Sept. 30,
Rt. 9 and Walkley Hill   Sat. & Sun. 2-5; free
Haddam—Phone 345-2400   admission, brochure.

The Amasa Day House (1816)

It is located at the junction of Routes 149 and 151 on the green in the center of Moodus. While little information has been found regarding the early history of the house it is known to have been built in 1816 by Julius Chapman. In 1843 Amasa Day, visiting Moodus, bought the house and property at an auction and lived there until his death in 1896 at age 88. In 1878 Mr. Day enlarged the original kitchen, added a modern one and at the same time built the conservatory.

One of the unusual features of the house are the original stencilled designs to be seen today on the front stairs, the upstairs hallway and on two floors. These were said to have been "laid on" by Mrs. Chapman shortly after the house was built. These designs are considered so unusual that they have been illustrated in several books on American decorative painting and copied for the Index of American Design in the Smithsonian Institution in Washington, D.C.

The house has been furnished almost entirely with three generations of Day family heirlooms that were acquired with the house. These heirlooms which mainly span the years from about 1800 through the 1840's have been displayed in seven museum rooms, each one restored with appropriate period colors and fabrics. An outstanding example of Connecticut craftsmanship to be seen is a rare cherry blockfront chest of drawers, one of two known; the other is in the Henry Francis duPont Winterthur Museum in Delaware.

In addition to fine examples of furniture there are noteworthy collections of ceramics, wrought-iron, children's toys, mirrors and clocks.

Antiquarian & Landmarks Society, Inc.   Open: daily May 15 to
   of Connecticut   Oct. 15, 1-5.
Moodus—Phone 873-8144   50¢

Florence Griswold House (1817)

The Florence Griswold House, a Greek Revival structure of graceful proportions with four Ionic columns, was designed and built by Colonel Samuel Belcher, a shipwright-architect in 1817. Adapting Christopher Wren designs, Belcher, in the same year, built the Fourth Meeting House, subject of four famous paintings by Childe Hassam, before it burned in 1907.

Built originally for William Noyes, the house was bought by Captain Robert Griswold in 1841, and was the birthplace of Miss Florence Griswold. "Miss Florence" housed, fed and entertained the group of Lyme painters, led by Henry W. Ranger, discoverer of the ideal Lyme landscapes that later brought the struggling art colony to fame and lasting historical importance.

The house, now the headquarters of the Lyme Historical Society, is part of Old Lyme's Historical District and was appointed to the National Register of Historic Places in 1971. The Society's collections include paintings and panels left by the artists, the extensive Mac-Curdy-Salisbury china collection, dolls, early household effects, tools, quilts, costumes, furnishings and rugs of museum quality.

Intimately associated in the life of the historic group were, among many others, Childe Hassam, Willard Metcalf, Carleton and Guy Wiggins, Clark G. Voorhees; "guests" of Miss Florence, comprising the gayest, hardest-working artists' paradise New England has ever produced.

Lyme Historical Society
Exit 70, Conn. Tpke, next
 building north of Lyme Art Gallery
Old Lyme—Phone 434-5542

Open: daily during summer months 10-12, 1-5, Sundays 1-5, closed Mon. After Labor Day, by appt. 50¢, children under 12, 25¢.

The Thomas Lee House (c. 1660)

Seven English sovereigns were recognized by the Lee family who occupied this house, beginning with Ensign Thomas Lee II, whose single room dwelling was constructed around 1660. As the family grew, the house was enlarged, two rooms being added about 1695, and further additions, 1730-35, brought it to its present form—a center chimney, saltbox type, reputed to be the oldest frame structure in the state and generally recognized for its interesting architectural details.

Changes were made over the years, but in 1914 it was restored by Norman Morrison Isham, noted authority on Connecticut architecture, for the East Lyme Historical Society. A classic cornice extends across the front and the entrance door is surmounted by five small window lights. The earliest, or east room is sheathed vertically with shadow-molded boards. The west rooms are plastered and panelled.

The Lee family held important posts in the colonial days. Ensign Thomas was a land holder, constable, head of the Train Band, and member of the General Assembly in 1676. His son John was author of "Dying Charge." John's son, John, was king's attorney, and another son, Joseph was author of the Lee genealogy. Thomas Lee III was a local justice for more than 40 years, and the Lee house was his seat of judgment.

The furnishings in the rooms reflect the growth of the family over a period of 250 years. The Little Boston School House, founded in 1734, is usually considered to be the first district school between New York and Boston. It is located on the property, and is included in the tour of the Lee House.

East Lyme Historical Society, Inc.
Shore Rd., Rt. 156
   opp. Bride Brook Rd.
East Lyme—Phone 739-6070

Open: daily except Tues.,
10-5, May 30-Oct. 12.
75¢, teens 25¢,
children 10¢

The Hempsted House (1678 & 1728)

The Hempsted family had resided in their homestead for almost a hundred years when Benedict Arnold landed with his British forces, and burned most of New London in 1781, but fortunately the Hempsted House survived. After its occupancy by ten generations of the family, it stands today, both in its architecture and period furnishings, as one of the finest of colonial dwellings.

Robert Hempsted was the first of the family to settle in New London, coming there from Long Island. He, with several others, received a grant of land in 1645 and may have built an earlier house.

Few houses have such a carefully documented history, thanks to the diary of Joshua Hempsted II, with the result that not only definite periods of the house are known, but types of furnishing as well. The west portion of the house was built by Joshua Hempsted I in 1678, while the newer, or eastern portion, was added by his grandson, Nathaniel, in 1728. During the next two hundred years, changes were made in the structure, but after its acquisition in 1938 by the Antiquarian & Landmarks Society, a very careful study was made, resulting in a most painstaking restoration.

In furnishing the museum, full use was made of notations in the diary, and many masterpieces in very early furnishings have been used, including some from the Hempsted family. There are numerous rarities in wrought iron, wooden ware, pewter and brass, simple cupboards and chests, Queen Anne tables, Bible box, candle stands, Carver chairs, early Connecticut tables, early hand spun and woven materials, and even a primitive baby walker and a folding bed.

Antiquarian & Landmarks Society, Inc.   Open: daily May 15 to
    of Connecticut   Oct. 15, 1-5
11 Hempsted Street   50¢
New London—Phone 443-7949

The Shaw Mansion (1756)

Connecticut's Naval Office during the Revolutionary War was located at the home of Captain Nathaniel Shaw and his son, Nathaniel, Jr., the latter having been appointed Naval Agent, successfully accomplishing the enormous task of providing ships, provisions, arms and money for the troops.

Captain Shaw, who came to New London about 1722, started a career sailing vessels from this port. He soon became a master and owner, and his successful ventures enabled him to establish a lucrative mercantile business. In January 1756 a shipload of dispossessed Acadians from Nova Scotia reached the port and Captain Shaw helped with rehabilitation by engaging thirty-five of them to quarry stone from his land and build his house.

When Benedict Arnold burned New London in 1781, fires were set in the building, but it was saved by prompt action of the neighbors. During the 19th century the house was considerably altered; a porch was added and a stone wing built where the original wooden kitchen had been. The Society is now restoring a great part of the Mansion to its original appearance, opening up Colonial fireplaces and discovering panelled cement walls.

Members of the Shaw family owned the property until 1907, when it was purchased by the New London County Historical Society. Numerous pieces of furniture owned by the Shaws, as well as silver, china and books are on display. There is also a superb collection of letters and manuscripts. The room that was once occupied by General George Washington is maintained as a memorial.

New London County Historical Society   Open: Tues.-Sat. 1-4.
11 Blinman Street   50¢, children 25¢ when
New London—Phone 443-1209   accompanied by adult.

Deshon-Allyn House (1829)

Of unusual charm and distinction, the Deshon-Allyn House, located on the grounds of the Lyman Allyn Museum, was built in 1829 by Captain Daniel Deshon, prosperous and prominent whaling master. It represents the elegance and character of the late Federal period. Though the architect is not known, many of the interesting interior details were taken from the handbooks of Asher Benjamin.

The exterior is of massive granite construction, the corners edged with finished stone quoins. Beneath the eaves a heavy, carved cornice is carried around the building. The six-panel front door is flanked by sidelights and topped with a square transom. The mullions are carved wood, ornamented with lead palmettes. The same treatment is applied to a beautifully executed Palladian window above the front door.

With a large central hall and four square rooms on each floor, each room contains a fireplace, four of which are original. The others are characteristic of the Federal period, including a black marble one, installed when the Hillhouse Mansion in New Haven was torn down. The house is furnished as of 1829 with furniture and decorative accessories from the Lyman Allyn Museum collections, all outstanding pieces. The portraits, landscapes and other pictures on display are in keeping with the era.

The house was purchased in 1851 by another prosperous whaler, Captain Lyman Allyn, and was occupied by the Allyn family until its acquisition by the Museum.

Lyman Allyn Museum   Open: Tues.-Fri. 1-5,
613 Williams Street   upon request to the
New London—Phone 443-2545   Museum.

Denison Homestead (1717)

This famous mansion is unique in two respects. It was restored by J. Frederick Kelly in successive periods: 1717 kitchen; 1775 and 1860 bedrooms; 1810 and 1910 parlors. It is authentically furnished throughout with family heirlooms; all floor coverings, pictures and furniture were always at home here. The house gives a realistic view of daily life with examples of the various "modernizations" made to meet changing living conditions through eleven generations.

Capt. George Denison, veteran of Cromwell's army and later commander of Connecticut troops in King Phillip's War, built a log lean-to, encircled with a palisade, and after the Indian wars, his "mansion hous." It burned and the next year, 1717, his grandson, George III, built the present house on the same site.

The collections of family heirlooms are exceptionally interesting because they include so many unusual items. Among them are Capt. George's will in his own writing, his bullet mold, samples of his wife's needlework, a king-size mortar and pestle made by an Indian slave, homemade crow decoys and a jointed wooden doll with rabbit fur hair, a camphorwood sea chest and Civil War carpetbag. In the kitchen, the wooden dishes, pewter ware and cooking utensils are notable.

Across the road 125 acres of the original Dension land-grant are maintained with miles of scientifically labeled Nature Trails and a new Museum by the Pequot-sepos Wildlife Sanctuary. Open free with guides.

The Denison Society, Inc.   Open: daily except
Pequotsepos Avenue   Mon., May 15-Nov. 1,
Mystic—Phone 536-9248   1-5; winter by appoint.
                                             75¢, children 6-15, 25¢

Samuel Buckingham House (1768)

No more fitting location could be found for a typical colonial dwelling than in the midst of Mystic Seaport Village, to which site it was transported by barge from Old Saybrook. Erected by Samuel Buckingham in 1768 and attached to a smaller ell probably built around 1690 by Samuel's grandfather, the Rev. Thomas Buckingham, the house is an outstanding example of mid-18th century architecture.

Sturdily constructed, the house has two stories and attic, plastered walls and a huge central chimney which serves a fireplace in each room. The first floor north room, with its classic wallpaper, is furnished in the period of 1770 to 1790, with a fine Queen Anne desk, Spanish-leather chair, paintings of 17th century ships, pine table and other period items. In the dining room is a corner cupboard containing a collection of pewter, as well as table, chairs and accessories of the period. Canopy beds, pine bureaus and early chairs are among the furnishings of the bedrooms.

Most striking is the kitchen ell, built about 1690, completely restored with great fireplace, pine sheathed walls, huge summer beam, leaded casement windows and other details, which with the furnishings, accurately portray a 17th century room. Here, it is alleged, took place the "battle of books," when Thomas Buckingham, as custodian of the library refused to release it for removal to New Haven, when Yale Collegiate School was transferred to that town from its earlier site in Old Saybrook.

Marine Historical Association
Mystic Seaport, Route 27
Mystic—Phone 536-2631

Open: daily 9-5, $3.50
and $1.50; winter 10-4,
$3.00 and $1.25

Whitehall Mansion (1771-1775)

Whitehall Mansion, an eighteenth century country mansion recently restored and authentically furnished by the Stonington Historical Society, was built in the years 1771-1775 by Dr. Dudley Woodbridge, a prosperous Groton physician, as a suitable setting for his retirement.

Gambrel-roofed, with three-foot cedar shingles, the house has 12 over 12 window lights on both floor levels. The panelling, most of which is original, is far more handsome than that found in the usual New England farmhouse, with cornices and panelled wainscoting in every room, and turned balusters at the front stairway. The massive chimney is brick from the first floor to the attic; in the kitchen (thought to be part of a much earlier house on the site) the huge fireplace has a rare brick "trimmer arch" to support the hearthstone of a fireplace in the room upstairs. The ceilings in the rooms both up and downstairs are unusually high for a country home.

In its history, the mansion passed through many hands. The last to own and live there was Florence Grace Bentley Keach, who donated the house in 1962 to the Stonington Historical Society, when it was moved to its present site to avoid demolition. The restoration was carried out in an authentic manner, and included a modern caretakers' wing. The upper rooms are believed to be identical in design and color scheme to that which existed in the latter days of Dr. Woodbridge's life. The house has been furnished in keeping with the style of the mansion.

Stonington Historical Society
Route 27
Stonington

Open: daily except
Saturdays, 2-4.
75¢

Leffingwell Inn (c. 1675)

Colonial New England reflected with charm and fidelity.

Rescued from superhighway bulldozers, moved and restored, the Leffingwell Inn delights antiquarian experts and classes of school children alike. It is definitely different. "The last word in restoration: so beautifully presented and full of interest," says Henry F. DuPont of Winterthur, and visitors from every state and as far away as Sweden and China exclaim: "Most interesting house we've seen." Leffingwell Inn has a threefold interest.

History: In 1701 Thomas Leffingwell was "granted liberty by the town to keep a publique house of entertainment for strangers" in his home which, during the Revolution, became local headquarters for patriots. Thomas' grandson, Christopher, collected supplies for the Continental Army, and was a pioneering industrialist, establishing the first paper and knitting mill in Connecticut, a pottery, dye house and chocolate mill.

Architecture: Connecticut colonists sometimes joined two small houses to make a mansion and then went on adding ells. The Inn evolved in this manner and its restoration reveals clearly these thrifty habits.

Museum: Unusually fascinating collections of pewter, silver, swords and clocks made by Norwich craftsmen; kitchen, dairy and farm implements; local Indian relics including a carved wooden succotash bowl, and rare furniture, such as the twin of the three-cornered presidential chair of Harvard.

Society of the Founders of Norwich,
  Connecticut, Inc.
Exit 81, Conn. Tpke., Rts. 2 & 32
Norwich—Phone 889-9440

Open: May 16-May 31,
2-4; June 1-Labor Day,
10-12, 2-4; Labor Day to
Oct. 15, 2-4; Oct. 16-
May 15, Sat. & Sun. 2-4.
Closed Mon. all year.

Rockwell House (1818)

While not as old as some of the historic buildings of Norwich, the imposing gray stone Rockwell House, built in 1818 by Joseph Perkins, is one of particular interest because of the many fine items which are on display here. For many years this was the home of one of the city's leading physicians, Dr. John A. Rockwell, son-in-law of Joseph Perkins. Later, to preserve the house for future generations, his granddaughter, Mrs. Rockwell Cole, deeded it to Faith Trumbull Chapter, DAR. After some changes and improvements made with the approval of the donor, it is now maintained by that organization.

The east room, now the dining room, was an addition to the house, and the door leading to it from the hall was the original back door. A porch was also a later addition, while Dr. Rockwell added a room at the back to be used by him as an office, with outside entrance. This room now contains a display of early kitchen utensils, tools and other items.

Generous contributions by members of the chapter and friends have been received. Noteworthy among the exhibits in the house is an exceptionally large Franklin stove, early American furniture, an Ebenezer Tracy Windsor chair, unusual china and glass, old wedding dresses and other costumes, early hat boxes, a trundle bed, rare crewel work, fans, hand embroidered infants' clothing and children's toys of fascination to members of much earlier generations.

Faith Trumbull Chapter, DAR
42 Rockwell Street
Norwich—Phone 887-8737

Open: Wed. 2-5,
July and August,
and by appointment.

Nathaniel Backus House (1750)

Nathaniel Backus, the grandson and great grandson of two William Backuses who were founders of Norwich, built his home in 1750 on a site facing the well travelled highway, now lower Broadway, with its back overlooking the old swamp. Here the house stood for two hundred years, when it was moved to its present site on Rockwell Street.

The Backus family was not only prominent in Norwich, but their activities were closely connected with the Trumbulls in Lebanon with some of whom they shared church pews in the earliest meeting house in Norwich.

The house retains some of its original and interesting features, among which are the heavy front door, flanked by pillars and rosettes, and its early staircase with round rail, hand carved corner newel posts and decorated treads.

Like the Rockwell House next door, the Backus House is the property of Faith Trumbull Chapter, DAR, and is also maintained as a museum. Here are found furniture and works of art, rare old glass and china, ancient Chinese sewing table, rose jars, various chairs of historic connection, as well as a table used by John Trumbull, the artist, for mixing paints. Also there are two pastel portraits of the 1790's by Sarah Perkins—one of an unkown boy, the other of an unknown girl. The portraits were found in the attic of the Rockwell House.

Faith Trumbull Chapter, DAR   Open: Wed. 2-5 in
42 Rockwell Street   July and August,
Norwich—Phone 887-8737   and by appointment.

Governor Jonathan Trumbull House (1735-40)

Governor Jonathan Trumbull was the only colonial governor who supported American independence. His home, built by his father, Captain Joseph Trumbull, was moved a short distance to its present site in 1830. Besides conducting the affairs of the state, the war governor supplied men and great quantities of munitions and food for the army.

The front entrance and the lower tier of front windows with pedimented heads and molded sills are noteworthy. Inside, the heart shaped penetrations of the shutters, the main stairway, the three chimneys converging into a single stack, and the panelling are of great interest. Recent restoration disclosed the location of a hidden staircase, believed to be the one down which John Trumbull, son of Jonathan and noted painter, fell when a child, losing the sight of an eye. Another staircase led from the governor's office to a tunnel leading to the War Office.

The house is furnished with authentic antiques, all ante-dating 1830, many of which belonged to the Trumbull family. The latter includes a Queen Anne chair, Hepplewhite chair, Chinese lacquer dispatch box, and china with a medallion in gray of a bull with head turned to one side. Among the guests frequenting the house were Generals Washington, Knox, Putnam, Marquis de Lafayette, Count de Rochambeau and Benjamin Franklin.

In 1954 the Wadsworth stable, a building of pure Grecian Palladian architecture, was moved from Hartford to the property.

Connecticut Daughters of the
  American Revolution
Second house N. of Main St. &
  Colchester Road
Lebanon—Phone 642-7558

Open: May 1-Nov. 1,
Tues.-Sat., 1-5,
50¢

The Nathan Hale Homestead (1776)

Nathan Hale has long been considered one of the country's outstanding heroes, and while it is doubtful he ever lived in the house, his name is closely associated with it. He was born in an earlier house that once stood nearby, part of which is now the present ell of the Homestead. His father, Deacon Richard Hale, was building his new house during the Revolution and moved into it with his family about a month after Nathan was hanged as a spy by the British, September 22, 1776.

The Homestead was one of the mansion houses of the area when it was built, although according to accurate records, it was not all completed at one time, and the rear sections of the ell were added at later dates.

Since the acquisition of the house by the Antiquarian & Landmarks Society, many splendid gifts have been received, including many pieces that were the property of the Hale family—furniture, portraits, a Burnap clock, china, pewter, tools, Nathan Hale's boyhood gun, his silver shoe buckles and Bible. One of the rooms was used as a school where Nathan's brother, David, taught the children of the neighborhood; another was the Judgment room, where Deacon Hale, and later various sons presided as justices of the peace. The rooms are appropriately furnished with period pieces, and the curtains and bed furnishings are original home spun, handwoven materials.

Joanna Hale was a sister of Nathan. Her rare English pewter plates with her name inscribed on them, her lovely china, her creamware vases, and some of her costumes are among the treasured heirlooms.

Antiquarian & Landmarks
  Society, Inc. of Connecticut
South Street, accessible from
  Rts. 6 to 44A
Coventry—Phone 742-6917

Open: May 15 to Oct. 15,
1-5 daily; $1.00

Henry C. Bowen House (1846) (Roseland Cottage)

This imposing board and batten Gothic Revival summer "cottage" was built for the famed Brooklyn, New York publisher and owner of "The Independent." The architect was Joseph C. Wells of New York City. This is one of New England's most important surviving examples of the Gothic Revival.

Containing many of its original furnishings, including several pieces designed by the architect, the house has always been lived in by the Bowen family. The grounds and extensive out-buildings include one of the earliest private bowling alleys in this country, and a Classical style garden house adjacent to the landscaped, boxwood gardens.

Presidents Grant, Hayes, Harrison and McKinley were guests at Roseland on various of its celebrated Fourth of July festivities. The house was acquired with the assistance of the Connecticut Historical Commission.

Society for the Preservation of
    New England Antiquities
Rt. 169, facing Woodstock Common
Woodstock

Open: June-Oct., Tues.,
Thurs. & Sat. 1-5.
$2.00 (Conn. residents,
$1.00)

1   Putnam Cottage, rendering by Robert Carter, Architect, 'Essex, Conn.
10 Eells Stow House, courtesy Conn. Development Commission
11 Stephen Ford House, Gutrick of Milford
19 Glebe House, Peter R. Lucas
22 Deacon Peter Buell House, Don Ereminas
24 Solomon Rockwell House, Clinton Studio, Winsted
31 Oliver Ellsworth House, Hartford Times
32 Cheney Homestead, Reginald Pinto, Manchester, Conn.
33 Mark Twain House, Mark Twain Memorial, Hartford, Conn.
34 Harriet Beecher Stowe House, Stowe-Day Foundation, Hartford, Conn.
37 Stanley-Whitman House, W. F. Miller & Co.
40 Buttolph-Williams House, Louis H. Frohman
41 Joseph Webb House, Robert L. Nay
42 Isaac Stevens House, Robert L. Nay
43 Silas Deane House, Hartford Courant
44 Welles-Shipman-Ward House, Duffy (Mrs. Gerhard R. Schade, Jr.),
     Glastonbury, Conn.
45 General Mansfield House, Stekl
46 Andrews Homestead, Allen E. Myers
50 Henry Whitfield House, Sedge LeBlanc
52 Thomas Griswold House, Richard Chapman
53 Nathaniel Allis House, courtesy Conn. Development Commission
54 Adam Stanton House, courtesy Conn. Development Commission
56 Stone House, Stekl
59 Florence Griswold House, Lincoln McCabe
61 Hempsted House, Louis H. Frohman
62 Shaw Mansion, Robert L. Perry
64 Denison Homestead, courtesy Conn. Development Commission
71 Nathan Hale Homestead, Louis H. Frohman
72 Henry Bowen House, Jack E. Boucher, Linwood, N.J.